THE
LUCKY
FEW

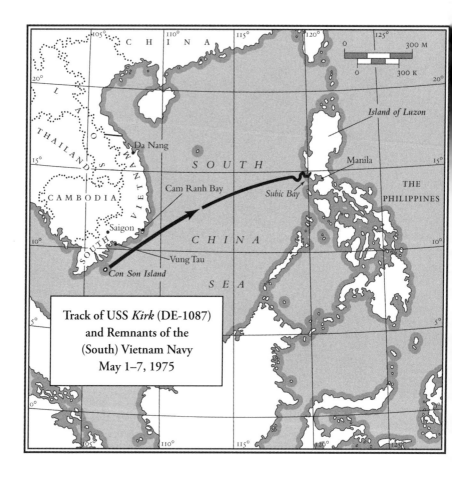

Track of USS *Kirk* (DE-1087)
and Remnants of the
(South) Vietnam Navy
May 1–7, 1975

THE
LUCKY
FEW

The Fall of Saigon and the
Rescue Mission
of the USS *Kirk*

JAN K. HERMAN

Naval Institute Press
Annapolis, Maryland

Naval Institute Press
291 Wood Road
Annapolis, MD 21402

First Naval Institute Press paperback edition published in 2015.
ISBN: 978-1-61251-894-7 (paperback)
ISBN: 978-1-61251-335-5 (eBook)

The Library of Congress has cataloged the hardcover edition as follows:
Herman, Jan K., author.
  The lucky few : the fall of Saigon and the rescue mission of the USS Kirk / Jan K. Herman.
    pages cm
  Includes bibliographical references and index.
  Summary: "As the Vietnam War reached its tragic climax in the last days of April 1975, a task force of U.S. Navy ships cruised off South Vietnam's coast. The Lucky Few focuses on the role of USS Kirk in the rescue of not only the remnants of the South Vietnamese fleet but also 32,000 refugees fleeing from Communist forces to the safety of the Seventh Fleet ships offshore. Although the Vietnam War ended in chaos and shame, the epic story of USS Kirk and her success in rendering humanitarian assistance under inconceivable circumstances is one of America's shining military involvements. The Lucky Few brings to light this relatively unknown heroic tale of a people caught up in the death throes of a nation and their subsequent passage to freedom"— Provided by publisher.
  ISBN 978-0-87021-039-6 (hardcover : alk. paper) — ISBN 978-1-61251-335-5 (ebook) 1. Kirk (Destroyer escort) 2. Vietnam War, 1961–1975—Naval operations, American. 3. Vietnam War, 1961–1975—Vietnam—Ho Chi Minh City. 4. Operation Frequent Wind, 1975. 5. Humanitarian assistance, American—Vietnam—Ho Chi Minh City. I. Title.
  DS558.7.H46 2013
  959.704'3450973—dc23
                                                                        2013025851

♾ Print editions meet the requirements of ANSI/NISO z39.48-1992 (Permanence of Paper).
Printed in the United States of America.

23 22 21 20 19 18 17 16 15   9 8 7 6 5 4 3 2

To the officers and men of USS *Kirk*
and the many "Lucky Few" they brought to freedom

CONTENTS

PREFACE

I N 2009 I completed the final book in a trilogy about Navy medicine's participation in World War II, the Korean War, and the Vietnam War. *Navy Medicine in Vietnam*[1] tells the story of my generation's war. The last chapter, "Full Circle," focuses on the humanitarian task that Navy medical personnel played in caring for the thousands of refugees who fled South Vietnam when that nation ceased to exist.

As the war reached its tragic climax in the last days of April 1975, a task force of U.S. Navy ships cruised off South Vietnam's coast. Its mission was to support the evacuation of Americans—embassy personnel and military advisers. But the task force was also assigned to secure the safety of "sensitive" South Vietnamese who had helped the United States during the war and whose lives would be in danger once the North Vietnamese consolidated their victory. But how best to record the stories of those who took care of these people now without a country?

After determining the names of the ships comprising Seventh Fleet Task Force 76, I did what every researcher does nowadays: go to the Internet. I checked every ship name to determine what vessels might have reunion organizations, knowing that their websites would provide contact names and e-mail addresses. The next step was e-mailing each organization to request information about medical personnel from those ships. Within an hour of hitting "send," I received a call from Capt. Paul Jacobs, former CO (commanding officer) of USS *Kirk*. He informed me that his ship, a destroyer escort, had not only been a part of that task force, but *Kirk* had played a key role in the rescue of more than 30,000 Vietnamese refugees.

"I'd like to interview members of *Kirk's* medical department," I said, trying to conceal mounting enthusiasm in my voice. "Do you have their names and contact information?" He laughed, exclaiming, "Medical department! We had two corpsmen aboard—a chief and a third class."

During the next several weeks, Jacobs and I communicated frequently. We arranged for an oral history interview at his office. Before long, I was phoning or e-mailing other members of the crew, including retired Stephen Burwinkel, *Kirk*'s chief hospital corpsman. Jacobs then invited me to the ship's reunion, scheduled to be held in suburban Northern Virginia that October of 2007.

"If I invited the surgeon general, do you think he would come as our guest speaker?" Jacobs inquired. "Send him an invitation. What do you have to lose?" I responded. Shortly thereafter, Vice Adm. Adam Robinson, brand-new to his job as surgeon general of the Navy, questioned me about the invitation, the nature of the *Kirk* reunion, and why this ship was so special. I told him what I knew and that the event, as I understood it, would be well worth attending. His curiosity got the better of him and he accepted.

The reunion was highly emotional. Former *Kirk* sailors and officers and once dispossessed Vietnamese saw each other for the first time since the end of the Vietnam War. When introduced to give his after-dinner remarks, the surgeon general tossed the written text aside. Touched by the poignant human drama he had witnessed that evening, he pointed out that his prepared speech was no longer appropriate. He then spoke spontaneously from the heart about *Kirk* and what her crew had accomplished in saving so many lives thirty-two years before. Their selfless acts of compassion were in the best traditions of providing humanitarian assistance to those in need and were an example of what the U.S. Navy does best.

Following the reunion, Vice Admiral Robinson invited Captain Jacobs and me to lunch at his Bureau of Medicine and Surgery headquarters in Washington, D.C.

During the salad course, the admiral turned to me and said, "Jan, you make documentaries. You must make a film about the *Kirk*. People have to know about this incredible story." I nodded my assent, not knowing whether or not this was idle lunchtime chatter. During dessert, I asked the admiral if he was serious about me producing a film. Looking directly at me as only a three-star admiral can, he said firmly and unequivocally, "Would I have suggested it if I weren't serious?"

Hours later, after the necessary paperwork had been completed, the surgeon general affixed his signature and *The Lucky Few* documentary project was under way. More than two years of challenging research followed, but the project was also a labor of love. I spent countless hours poring through *Kirk*'s logs and other documents and writing and rewriting the script. Then my director, Tom Webster, his staff from Navy Medicine Support Command,

and I traveled around the country interviewing members of *Kirk*'s crew, former Vietnamese refugees, and other related players caught up in this last act of war. We assembled all the components, which included their on-camera interviews, photographs loaned to us by the crew, and historical footage obtained from the National Archives, Navy collections, and ABC News VideoSource. Finally, we recorded the narration and began editing the documentary.

At the *Kirk* reunion in July 2010, with Vice Admiral Robinson again in attendance, we showed *The Lucky Few: The Story of USS* Kirk *Providing Humanitarian & Medical Care at Sea*. Shortly thereafter, National Public Radio aired several stories about *Kirk*'s humanitarian assistance. That three-part NPR series won national acclaim. On Veterans Day, November 11, 2010, *The Lucky Few* premiered at the Smithsonian Institution's Baird Auditorium in Washington, D.C.

It became obvious to me and other interested parties that a one-hour film could scarcely do justice to this previously untold story. Why had the incident been overlooked for so many years? The answer most likely had to do with America's mood in 1975. The national nightmare of Vietnam was over and it was time to move on. The unpopular conflict that had torn the nation asunder as no other since the Civil War, was best left forgotten. Moreover, the men of *Kirk* and crewmen of other ships who had participated in the rescue never thought they had done anything extraordinary. Feeding refugees and diapering infants were not war-related duties that warriors felt worth sharing with old buddies in American Legion or VFW halls—and they didn't discuss these humanitarian experiences with family and friends. Not surprisingly, most former refugees had not passed on their memories to children and grandchildren. More than thirty years had not softened the trauma of loss of country and loss of lives.

The gatherings, which enabled many of those *Kirk* sailors and officers to mingle with former refugees, rekindled memories and emotions too long suppressed. The dynamics of those reunions were profound. Joseph Pham, a former refugee rescued by *Kirk*, observed during one gathering that he counted himself "among the lucky few" and wanted to express his deep sense of gratitude to the people who had saved and brought him and his family to freedom. Like Pham, other Vietnamese—who had made new lives for themselves and their families as Americans—were able to personally thank the rescuers who had made their passage to freedom possible.

And seeing the tangible results of their wartime duty, the men of USS *Kirk* could now take pride in what they had accomplished. *The Lucky Few* experience—with accompanying national recognition—led many of *Kirk*'s former crewmen to judge their Vietnam service in a totally new light. They now realized that they, too, were among "the lucky few" to take part in such an epic human drama.

Donald Cox, a former airman attached to *Kirk*'s helicopter detachment, put those thoughts into perspective: "Our feelings about being in Vietnam had changed significantly. We had gone to Vietnam with expectations of being in combat. We were prepared for it. We were trained for it. And that was the action we were looking for. When we got there, we found out that combat wasn't what was needed. It was a heart and hand that was needed. We didn't recognize it at first. We just did our jobs. It was afterward that we realized our Vietnam experience was totally different from our brothers who had walked in the field in combat. We recognized that it was going to be a positive experience for the rest of our lives. We were there to save life and not to destroy it."

Writing a book based on *The Lucky Few* documentary offered new opportunities to tell as much of the story as possible and also to incorporate what had unfortunately ended up on the proverbial "cutting-room floor." In most Hollywood films, the book comes first followed by the movie. I would reverse the order with the advantage of adding flesh to the bones of an already larger-than-life event.

Despite *Kirk*'s valiant efforts, the rescue of the Republic of Vietnam Navy (VNN) was anything but a "Lone Ranger" operation. Although *Kirk* took the lead in feeding and providing water to more than 30,000 refugees during their odyssey across the South China Sea, that job was far too big an undertaking for just one destroyer escort. Many other Navy vessels joined the flotilla to lend assistance in delivering food, water, fuel, rice, medical supplies, and the temporary loan of hospital corpsmen and a Navy physician. Those ships included *Kirk*'s sister ship, USS *Cook*, plus USS *Mobile*, USS *Vega*, USS *Tuscaloosa*, USS *Barbour County*, USS *Denver*, USS *Deliver*, USS *Abnaki*, USS *Flint*, and USS *Lipan*. And so this account of USS *Kirk* is their story as well.

JAN K. HERMAN
August 2012

ACKNOWLEDGMENTS

A FTER SHOWINGS OF *The Lucky Few*, the documentary that inspired this book, numerous viewers have asked how USS *Kirk* rated combat photographers among her crew. It would seem that the many color images, which so skillfully captured those dramatic events, were certainly created by professionals. But no such U.S. Navy photographers were assigned to the ship. Four crew members, James Bongaard, Kent Chipman, Craig Compiano, John Pine, and Hugh Doyle—all amateur shutterbugs—were responsible for taking the photographs, many of which appear in this volume. I am truly obliged to them for sharing these tangible "Kodachrome memories."

I would also like to express my thanks to all the officers and enlisted men who gave me their time to be interviewed at length. They could clearly recall their roles in that epic drama thirty-seven years ago—as if those events occurred just yesterday. Such lucid memories show that they must have realized they were caught up in something big.

I owe a huge debt of gratitude to Hugh Doyle for also reviewing portions of the manuscript for accuracy. He still has a discerning eye as *Kirk*'s former chief engineer. Given the nature of his duty on the ship, he was everywhere in the thick of the action.

I would also like to thank Vice Adm. Adam Robinson, former surgeon general of the Navy, for encouraging and supporting *The Lucky Few* documentary project. Without the film as a starting point, there would be no book.

And finally, I wish to thank the captain. I hold the highest appreciation and admiration for Paul Jacobs, the special force who even today still binds the men of USS *Kirk* together as he did during those tumultuous days of late April and early May 1975.

INTRODUCTION

L T. BOB LEMKE was up before dawn and wandered into USS *Kirk*'s Combat Information Center (CIC). As an aide on the Destroyer Squadron (DESRON) 23 staff, he was not a regular member of the crew and therefore had no business in CIC. "Combat" was always buzzing with activity, and it was not unusual for officers to pop in to relieve the boredom and catch up on the ship's operations. Amid the many radar scopes was a large radar repeater that consolidated information from the other displays. One look at the repeater screen put everything into perspective: distance to the South Vietnamese coast and the position of nearby vessels and their movements. Each green blip was a ship of some sort, making it easy to quickly see the location of every craft on a master grid.

But the screen image appeared odd. The shoreline was out of focus. Lemke pointed out the problem and asked a nearby tech if the radar had been tuned recently, thinking it might have lost some of its fidelity. The tech quickly responded, "Yes, sir, it has been. There's nothing wrong with the radar."[1]

Lemke wasn't satisfied. Going topside to the flying bridge, he grabbed the large binoculars—the "big eyes"—and scanned the brightening horizon. The mystery of the blurry radar screen instantly cleared up. Hundreds of boats were heading out to sea in *Kirk*'s direction. Lemke recalled, "The radar looked a little fuzzy only because there was so much activity on the water."[2]

As the distance closed, he noted every type of watercraft from small fishing vessels to rubber rafts. The lieutenant was shocked to see a tiny wooden dugout with a man, woman, and two children clinging for dear life. "On that dugout were all the family possessions, including a small motorbike. These people were simply paddling out to sea hoping to get to the rescue ships," he remembered.[3]

The magnitude of a nation's final collapse suddenly became real and personal. Since March 1975 the Army of the Republic of Vietnam (ARVN) had been hard pressed. The People's Army of Vietnam (PAVN) was now fighting a conventional war with tanks and artillery. The enemy was rolling south along Route 1 and taking every coastal city in its path. Names that had etched deep scars in the American psyche after years of war took the headlines: Hue, Danang, Qui Nhon, Cam Ranh Bay, Nha Trang. In the Central Highlands, several North Vietnamese divisions sliced eastward, eroding further what remained of South Vietnam. For days prior to the fall of Saigon, the by-products of that relentless conquest were thousands of panicked refugees trying to flee the country in anything that would float.

"It was Dunkirk in reverse," observed Paul Jacobs, USS *Kirk*'s CO at the time of this operation.[4]

On Tuesday, April 29, 1975, *Kirk*, a destroyer escort, was operating with Seventh Fleet Task Force 76, about twelve miles off the South Vietnamese coast near the port of Vung Tau. At the time, large CH-53 Sea Stallions and CH-46 Sea Knights began shuttling American and Vietnamese evacuees from Saigon to Task Force 76's aircraft carriers and amphibious assault ships. The helicopter evacuation known as Operation Frequent Wind had begun, and the final act of the Vietnam War was now at hand.

Quite unexpectedly, swarms of helicopters from the army of Vietnam and Vietnamese air force (VNAF) followed the American helos out to sea. Most were crammed with men, women, and children seeking refuge on board any of the forty-four U.S. Navy ships that offered a clear flight deck. Having advertised her hospitality over the air distress radio frequency, *Kirk* began taking some of the South Vietnamese helicopters on board her tiny flight deck.

Instantly, officers and sailors—trained as warriors—transformed a man-of-war, which had been designed to destroy Soviet submarines, into a humanitarian assistance ship. People who had lost everything, including their nation, found comfort, sustenance, and medical care on board *Kirk*. Desperation and anguish gave way to reassurance as crew members fed their unexpected guests, dispensed medical care, diapered infants, set up awnings to protect the refugees from a blazing sun, and provided hope to a dispirited people.

Had *Kirk* accomplished just that one operation, it would have been enough. But fate had yet another mission for this unlikely warship. For reasons still not fully understood almost four decades later, Task Force 76's commander ordered *Kirk* and her crew to return to Vietnam and lead the remnants of the Vietnamese navy to safety in the Philippines. *The Lucky Few* brings to light this virtually unknown episode of the Vietnam War and highlights one small ship's unexpected and heroic role in escorting thousands of refugees to freedom.

ONE

MAN-OF-WAR

O<small>N SEPTEMBER 25</small>, 1971, a destroyer escort (DE) decked out with festive pennants stood atop her launch crib in the Avondale Shipyard at Westwego, Louisiana. It had been nine months since the laying of her keel. Now with speeches and the obligatory smashing of a champagne bottle against the steel bow by her namesake's widow, the gray warship with hull number 1087 skidded sideward down the ways. She splashed into the Mississippi River, heeling well over to port before righting herself. The brand-new man-of-war carried the name of Vice Adm. Alan G. Kirk, senior U.S. naval commander during the June 1944 Normandy landings.[1]

Kirk would have many talents. The Cold War had not yet abated, and the ship's mission was to hunt, detect, and, if it became necessary should the Cold War turn hot, destroy Soviet submarines that might threaten U.S. Navy carrier task forces she was obliged to protect. Once Avondale's yard workers installed and tested her weapons systems, sonar, and radar equipment and made her ready for sea, *Kirk*'s nucleus crew, employed by the company, got her under way down to the Gulf of Mexico and steaming through the Caribbean.[2] She then transited the Panama Canal and headed north through Pacific waters to the Long Beach Naval Shipyard where several postconstruction modifications would be made. Before joining the U.S. Seventh Fleet, the fledgling also had to acquire her crew.

Kirk and her sister *Knox*-class DEs had a distinguished ancestry: DEs had performed yeoman service in World War II, especially during the Battle of the Atlantic. Crewed by 215 officers and men and averaging 300 feet in length, these scrappy little ships displaced roughly 1,700 tons fully loaded. The DEs were sometimes called the "poor man's destroyers" because of their size, armament, slower speed, and cost. DEs owed much of their design to British and Canadian corvettes that had already proven their worth not only for doing hazardous convoy duty in the North Atlantic but also as effective antisubmarine warships.

World War II DEs lacked big-gun offensive firepower, but they compensated for this gunnery deficit in their seaworthiness, maneuverability, and tenacity. Having a turning radius half that of a destroyer, a DE could stick to an underwater target like a hound to a fox's scent. With their complement of antisubmarine weaponry—sonar, surface search radar, depth charges, and an efficient means of delivering them—DEs were now part of efficient Hunter-Killer task groups. These search-and-destroy forces had proved especially deadly to German and Japanese submarines.

By the end of World War II, the newest generation of DEs carried two 5-inch, 38-caliber dual-purpose guns enclosed in rotatable gun mounts. In addition to these primary batteries, the more advanced DEs had a secondary battery of eight Oerlikon 20-mm rapid-fire guns and one quadruple 1.1-inch or one twin 40-mm Bofors antiaircraft gun.

For those ships whose primary role was antisubmarine warfare, stern-mounted depth charge racks and British-designed K-guns were essential equipment. The K-guns were launchers mounted on both sides of the ship that, when fired, propelled depth charges outward. Many of the newest DEs also had a Royal Navy–designed launcher called a "hedgehog," which fired a pattern of small mortar bombs from deck-mounted racks. Unlike depth charges, which required time or hydrostatic pressure–activated fuses or magnetic impulse detonators, these weapons exploded on contact. The DE had become one of the most versatile ships of World War II capable of performing many roles.

The Cold War required an even more sophisticated vessel to counter Soviet submarines. In the mid-1960s naval architects and marine engineers created the *Knox*-class DE, based on the most successful designs of post–World War II. The first vessel and namesake of the class, USS *Knox* (DE-1052), came off the ways in November 1966. By the time USS *Moinester* (DE-1097) joined the fleet eight years later, forty-six *Knox/Hewes*–class DEs had been built.[3]

Kirk, as her sisters, was a formidable warship. She measured 438 feet in length, had a 46-foot 9-inch beam, and displaced 4,250 tons fully loaded. At that displacement, the ship drew nearly twenty-five feet of water. The ship's deck gun was a 5-inch, 54-caliber rapid-fire cannon positioned in a forward mount and controlled by radar and a gunfire control system.

Kirk's below-the-waterline, bow-mounted sonar dome was her raison d'être—to detect submarines. A towed array sonar system aided in that mission. For close-in attack against submarines, the ship had four torpedo tubes built into the after superstructure, each firing the Mark 46 acoustically guided torpedo. For more distant underwater threats, her main sub-busting weapon was a forward deck–mounted, eight-tube ASROC (antisubmarine rocket) launcher. The detection of a hostile submarine would initiate the launch of one of the eight ASROCs. Its warhead was either an acoustic homing torpedo or a nuclear-tipped rocket-thrown depth charge (RTDC). The rocket then began its unguided ballistic trajectory toward the target. During that flight, the payload would separate from the missile and deploy a parachute to ease the torpedo or depth charge into the water at a relatively low velocity and with minimal noise. The water entry would then activate the torpedo and guide it toward the target by its own active or passive sonar. If the warhead were the RTDC, the unguided payload would sink quickly to a predetermined depth where it would detonate. Absolute precision for this weapon was not required.

Located amidships, the ship's command and control spaces—*Kirk*'s "brains" or nerve center—included the bridge, living quarters for the commanding officer (CO),[4] and the Combat Information Center (CIC). This massive superstructure combined the ship's mast and stack—"mack"—for boiler exhausts. Atop the mack were radar, radio, and electronic warfare antennas. The rotating radar antennas transmitted images to repeaters (radar screens) located in the CIC and on the bridge.

Just aft of the superstructure and one level above the main deck, *Kirk*'s modest flight deck with telescoping hangar accommodated a single SH-2F Seasprite LAMPS (Light Airborne Multi-Purpose System) helicopter. This versatile aircraft, with its highly trained crew, extended the ship's detection range by deploying acoustic sonobuoys and radar and magnetic anomaly detection (MAD) gear to locate submerged submarines. The aircraft could also search for other potential targets and—with its radar—provide early warning for antiship missiles and enemy ships or aircraft that might launch them.

Kirk's power plant, located below in her boiler and engine room spaces, consisted of two 1,275-psi boilers heated by high-quality kerosene called Navy distillate (ND). The resulting steam powered a single Westinghouse geared turbine, producing 35,000 shaft horsepower transmitted to her single five-bladed, 15-foot-diameter propeller. At twenty knots, the ship had a range of 4,500 nautical miles. With steam up on both boilers, she could exceed thirty knots. Technologically advanced for her day, *Kirk* had two gyro-controlled fin stabilizers that provided a more stationary platform for the launching of her ASROC and her LAMPS helicopter. A side benefit was a more comfortable ride for the crew in heavy seas.

Her freshwater evaporators could provide 24,000 gallons per day, a feature that in the future would be appreciated more than any seaman could imagine. The crew's quarters were the most advanced of the time, with air-conditioned berthing and messing spaces, a ship's store, barbershop, library, and galley.

The ship's complement of 22 officers and 270 enlisted was a young crew with the average age for the officers being approximately twenty-six, and the enlisted being twenty-three, with 85 crew members ranging in age from seventeen to twenty. For most *Knox/Hewes*-class DEs, the CO, also known as the captain, skipper, or, affectionately, "The Old Man," was a commander with at least fourteen years in the Navy before taking the helm.

The executive officer (XO) was the second in command, and his job was to execute the CO's decisions and orders for the ship. He was solely responsible for the day-to-day functioning of the command. While the principal department heads reported directly to the CO for mission-related operational matters, woe be to the officer who ignored or went around the XO on the way up to confer with the captain. The XO's main duty was to remain always ready to assume command at a moment's notice. While his day would be consumed by the maddening minutiae of the ship's routine, such as cleanliness, order, discipline, and habitability, he was first and always second in command, and that was at all times his primary concern.

The XO also supervised the Executive Department, which handled the ship's administration. Yeomen, personnelmen, and quartermasters staffed this department, as did the officer who was designated ship's navigator. Responsible for charting the ship's course, his duties included plotting the vessel's position and recommending optimal courses. His assistants were enlisted quartermasters responsible for maintaining the ship's navigational instruments, such as sextants, chronometers, and long range aid to navigation (LORAN), as well as maintaining the ship's chart locker. The ship's medical personnel also came directly under the XO.

The operations officer, usually assisted by three other officers, was responsible for the CIC, which housed repeaters, plotting and status display boards, and other equipment to provide the CO with an awareness of air, surface, and underwater situations. This department also oversaw the ship's electronic equipment and communications. This section was principally staffed by radarmen/operations specialists, radiomen, electronic warfare technicians, electronics technicians, and signalmen.

The Engineering Department, the largest department on board *Kirk*, operated and maintained the ship's main propulsion system, electrical generation systems, and auxiliary machinery. All mechanical, heating, air-conditioning, refrigeration, and electrical equipment (other than those systems specifically associated with weapons systems) came under this department. The engineer officer (chief engineer) and his two officer assistants directed ninety-three enlisted men with the rates of electrician's mate, engineman, interior communication electrician, boiler technician, machinist's mate, and hull technician.

The weapons officer supervised the three officers and sixty-six men of the Weapons Department, which was responsible for the maintenance and operation of the ship's 5-inch gun, ASROC launcher, torpedoes, and other weapons plus the two small boats (captain's gig and motor whaleboat). The Weapons Department maintained the cleanliness and preservation of all deck equipment and was also responsible for general line-handling. The Weapons Department included the enlisted rates of boatswain's mate, gunner's mate, fire control technician, sonarman, and torpedoman's mate.

The supply officer and his thirty-five enlisted men fulfilled the provision needs of the entire ship and crew, including food and its preparation and serving, clothing, pay, ship's stores, repair parts and spares, and the endless list of other items to maintain a man-of-war. The Supply Department's enlisted rates included storekeepers, disbursing clerks, ship's servicemen, and mess management specialists.

After completing her yard fitting, *Kirk* was commissioned on September 9, 1972, almost a year after her launch. She then joined the Cruiser-Destroyer Force, U.S. Pacific Fleet as a unit of Destroyer Squadron (DESRON) 23, made famous as Capt. Arleigh Burke's "Little Beavers" of World War II. Her home port was San Diego and later Yokosuka, Japan.

When *Kirk* rounded Point Loma and stood out to sea for her first Western Pacific (WESTPAC) deployment early in 1973, Cdr. Harold E. Burgess commanded a well-equipped, capable fighting machine, honed and ready to take on any Soviet submarine that might choose to get in her way.

TWO

THE OLD MAN

C APT. PAUL JACOBS is ruggedly built, standing six feet tall with military bearing and a smooth-shaven head, giving him a "Yul Brynner," resolute look. Still athletic and fit in his mid-seventies, he is precisely the unpretentious salty sea captain who earned his stripes upon the heaving decks of a Navy man-of-war. Yet his ready laugh and twinkling green eyes show a kindly man whose boundless enthusiasm, affection, and pride for his ship and crew have not diminished in the past thirty-five years. "I could ask that crew to do anything and they would do it," Jacobs called to mind decades later.[1] And, not surprisingly, that affection is mutual. Even today, the men of *Kirk*, now in late middle age, would certainly do anything for the man they still consider to be their skipper.

Cdr. Paul Jacobs was already an experienced officer with seventeen years in the Navy under his belt when he assumed command of USS *Kirk* in the summer of 1974. By that time he had served on board five ships—as XO of one and CO of two others. Unlike the many naval officers who came up through the Naval Academy, Jacobs received his education at the Maine Maritime Academy.

Jacobs seemed destined to earn his living as a seafaring man. Born in 1936 in Malden, Massachusetts, he moved with his family to his grandparents' farm in Cumberland Center, Maine, while he was still a young boy. With his father then serving in the Merchant Marine as a marine engineer for most of World War II, Paul's mother had her hands full raising three rambunctious boys and a girl. He fondly remembers his grandfather plowing the boulder-strewn New England ground as he dutifully followed closely behind, depositing seeds in the furrows.

The Jacobs family lived on the farm until Jacobs was ten, when his veteran father took a job as caretaker in the coastal community of Petit Manan Point where the family work ethic continued. It was a simple but rigorous life that seesawed between boyhood adventure—hunting and fishing—and plain hard work. "It was a tough life but you didn't have time to get into trouble," Jacobs remembered. "My brothers and I dug clams and raked blueberries, and that's how we made our money to buy clothes to go to school."[2]

A local farmer once gave the boy a heifer to raise as a pet. Jacobs went clamming one day and the animal followed him to the clamming flats. Taking advantage of the opportunity, the resourceful youth tied two burlap sacks of clams on her back to ease his own load. The neighbors had to smile when they saw the youngster return from the beach accompanied by his bovine beast of burden.

When his father began constructing a house for his brood, Jacobs and his brothers gleaned rocks from a nearby beach for a great fireplace. Although that fireplace may have turned out grand as intended, life in the modest house could still be austere. "We took our baths in a washtub in the middle of the kitchen," Jacobs recalled with a grin.[3] Without a doubt, that environment nurtured self-reliance, discipline, and personal responsibility—all characteristics Jacobs would display in his adult life.

When he graduated from tiny Milbridge High School in 1955, Jacobs entered the Maine Maritime Academy in nearby Castine with the intention of becoming a marine engineer as his father. Shortly after beginning his freshman semester, the fledgling midshipman noted that the academy was advertising for a professional marine engineer to teach engineering. He called his father to let him know about the job. The elder Jacobs soon became Professor George Jacobs who would show no favoritism toward his son.

"My father was harder on me than on the other midshipmen," the younger Jacobs recollected.[4] On one occasion, Midshipman Jacobs had been practicing lessons learned in the classroom by working all night repairing the steam plant on board the ex-Navy hospital ship USS *Comfort*. The training ship had been moored at the school pier as the TS *State of Maine*. The next morning, his father took him to task for his 8 a.m. shadow. "Being his son didn't matter one bit. He gave me extra duty for needing that shave."[5]

Jacobs graduated in 1958 and immediately went on active duty as an ensign in the Navy Reserve with orders to report on board USS *Onslow* (AVP-48), a seaplane tender. His knowledge and skills as an engineer officer did not go unnoticed or unrewarded. The ship's CO, Capt. Stockton Strong, noted in his fitness report that Jacobs' initiative and competence set him apart: "It has been gratifying to find in a young officer the leadership capability and intellectual honesty which he possesses."[6]

When Jacobs drew his next assignment on board the destroyer USS *Harry E. Hubbard* (DD-748), the newly promoted Lieutenant (junior grade) Jacobs became the ship's engineer officer, a highly unusual honor for such a junior officer.

Recognizing the young man's potential, his new CO understood that without mastering multiple skills, Jacobs would be forever typecast as an engineer and his Navy career a dead end. Moreover, Jacobs needed to become a regular naval officer (USN) and have the "R"—the Reserve designation—removed from the USNR title if he ever aspired to command his own ship. Reserve officers seldom assumed ship command during peacetime. Therefore, with that encouragement and advice and with the cooperation of the Bureau of Personnel, Jacobs transitioned into the regular Navy. He was temporarily assigned to the Fleet Gunnery School in San Diego to qualify him as weapons officer on *Harry E. Hubbard*, proficient in operating and maintaining the ship's 5-inch guns.

Besides, or even despite, his new title, Jacobs was determined to learn every aspect of the World War II–era destroyer. He crawled through her bilges and committed to memory every pipe and gauge in *Hubbard's* engine room. Before long, he could light off her boilers and fire her guns with equal skill. He could also ease the ship into a pier while fighting a headwind and crosscurrent. Shiphandling and seamanship were second nature since his Maine Maritime Academy days.

His personal skills were equally impressive. No artificial class barriers shielded Jacobs from the enlisted crew. He visited them in their workspaces, drank coffee with petty officers and non-rated sailors alike, spoke their language, shared their gripes and joys, and, most important, earned their respect. "You needed to know what they were thinking, not what you thought they were thinking," he remembered.[7] The gift of leadership, it seemed, was in Paul Jacobs' genes.

Lieutenant Jacobs detached from *Harry E. Hubbard* in early 1962 for a shore assignment—as a project officer overseeing the development of new navigation systems for Polaris ballistic missile-firing submarines (SSBNs). That duty took him to Syosset, New York, where the contractor Sperry Rand was developing and testing new systems on a full mock-up of an *Ethan Allen–* class fleet ballistic sub. His performance in this assignment cleared the way for his first sea command, USS *Meadowlark* (MSC-196), a 144-foot wooden-hull coastal minesweeper.[8] He set out to master an entire new set of skills and absorb a new glossary of terms—"sweep cables," "paravanes," and "pulse generators." He also had to learn the delicate art of explosive ordnance disposal.

Jacobs took to his first command with characteristic enthusiasm. *Meadowlark*, designed to clear coastal minefields, was powered by two diesel engines, and her new captain loved diesels. While a midshipman at Maine Maritime, Jacobs had spent hours tearing them down and reassembling them just for fun. Diesels were notoriously difficult to start, but once running they could continue to operate until they ran out of fuel.

One day a sister minesweeper, moored beside *Meadowlark*, could not get under way because her air compressor, essential for starting the engines, was out of order. Jacobs' experience with diesels paid off at this point. He hooked three 15-pound CO_2 bottles to the starboard engine's air cocks, and, with three well-timed blasts of carbon dioxide substituting for air, he then produced the required compression to start the engine. Jacobs next told the minesweeper's CO how to jump-start the port engine. With the disabled ship tied to *Meadowlark*'s starboard side, the two vessels headed down the channel. When they had reached about twelve knots, the port propeller began turning the shaft at the right speed, and the diesel engine turned over and started. The process was not unlike pushing a car with a manual transmission and then popping the clutch to engage the engine.

Lieutenant Jacobs had saved the day and enhanced his growing reputation as a "can-do" skipper. By the time he relinquished command in December 1965, after nearly two years as *Meadowlark*'s captain, the Navy had awarded the minesweeper her third and fourth Battle Efficiency awards.

Jacobs was due for another shore assignment, this time to advance his education at the Naval Postgraduate School in Monterey, California, and earn his bachelor of science degree. The school's courses were designed "to raise the educational level, broaden the mental outlook, and increase the professional and scientific knowledge."[9] While attending this school, he was promoted to lieutenant commander.

Graduation brought Jacobs a new sea command in 1967: captain of USS *Esteem* (MSO-438). This ship was an oceangoing minesweeper whose services were needed in Southeast Asia. Besides her primary task of minesweeping off the Vietnamese coast, *Esteem* occasionally provided gunfire support for American troops fighting ashore. "With our relatively shallow draft, we could get in close and fire our 40mm," Jacobs pointed out. "The troops could then tell us where we were hitting so we could adjust and fire for effect."[10]

An Army unit that was operating just south of the Demilitarized Zone (DMZ) once radioed the ship with a special request: to silence a North Vietnamese battery slightly north of the DMZ that had been harassing the soldiers for some time. *Esteem*'s 40-mm guns responded and took some enemy fire in return. Jacobs keenly recalled the enemy tracers streaking overhead.

Following two Vietnam combat tours on board *Esteem*, Jacobs drew another shore assignment, this time at the Naval War College in Newport, Rhode Island. He enrolled in the prestigious Command and Staff junior course. It was obvious he was being groomed for greater responsibility.

To a number of ambitious, hard-charging line officers, commanding a destroyer is the pinnacle of a Navy career. "Tin cans," as these rough-riding welterweights have affectionately been called over the years, are agile men-of-war—versatile and quick. Laden with guns, depth charges, and torpedoes, they are equally adept at hunting and killing submarines, providing gunfire support, and protecting a carrier task force from hostile aircraft. If Revolutionary War hero John Paul Jones was capable of time travel, without doubt he would return as the CO of a U.S. Navy destroyer.

"Not everybody can ride a tin can," Jacobs pointed out. "They bounce up and down and don't offer the smoothest ride. Yet there's a camaraderie and a sense of teamwork you don't find on other ships. When you're on a destroyer, you know everyone from the firemen all the way up to the captain. The crew is close and the men remain that way the rest of their lives. As an individual, you take pride in being a tin-can sailor."[11] At one point, while standing on *Meadowlark*'s bridge as the minesweeper headed out to sea, Jacobs saw a destroyer coming into port. "Doesn't that sight excite you and make you want to stay in the Navy?" he asked shipmate Rich Dobre, who noted his CO's visibly elevated mood.[12]

Before assuming command of his own tin can, Jacobs would first have to play understudy as XO of USS *Floyd B. Parks* (DD-884), a *Gearing*-class destroyer launched near the end of World War II. *Parks* offered Jacobs the kind of challenge he sought and an opportunity to practice everything he had learned to date—gunnery and shiphandling. With *Parks'* twin General Electric steam turbines and four boilers, Jacobs had been granted admission to marine engineers' paradise. *Parks* certainly represented an exponential leap from the world of wooden-hulled minesweepers.

Forty years later, his former CO, retired Navy captain James Donovan, recalled that Jacobs "worked very hard to keep the crew as a team and the crew responded very well to him."[13] As XO, Jacobs ran the ship's everyday operations. "We didn't always go by the book but ran the ship on common sense and Paul had a lot of that," Donovan called to mind.[14]

Not going by the book was and still is one of Jacobs' most observable traits. No one better adhered to the principle that "it's better to beg forgiveness than ask permission." In a rule-conscious and often hidebound Navy, this philosophy frequently meant the difference between failure and accomplishing the mission. When *Parks* deployed to South Vietnam for combat operations, Jacobs stepped beyond his XO role and volunteered to fly with and assist spotter aircraft over enemy territory to ensure that the destroyer's 5-inch shells landed on target.

Always conscious of his crew, he knew how to ease the tension and break the monotony. "Steel beach picnics" became a welcome diversion on board the destroyer when daily chores were momentarily set aside so the men could enjoy hamburgers and hotdogs on a deck masquerading as a white sand beach. Jacobs, as XO, was also responsible for crew morale. He once declared "Yahoo Day," convincingly telling the CO that this was a seafaring tradition inherited from Britain's Royal Navy. He authorized *Parks'* sailors to wear whatever they pleased as long as they performed their duties. A prize would then be awarded for the worst-dressed sailor. "Imagine my shock," Donovan recalled, "when a sailor, wearing nothing more than a coonskin cap and jockstrap, brought a message to me on the bridge!"[15]

When Lt. Cdr. James McCulloch, *Parks'* next skipper, unexpectedly had to leave the ship, he temporarily turned command over to Jacobs. "I had complete confidence that he would conduct the scheduled exercises. He took her out, did a good job, and brought the ship home. He told me later that I almost didn't get the keys back."[16]

A fatal helicopter accident propelled Jacobs toward his next assignment as plans officer serving with the Seventh Fleet's commander of Task Force 75. On May 8, 1972, Rear Adm. Rembrandt Robinson was killed, along with his chief of staff and operations officer. Their helicopter attempted a routine night landing when it crashed on board USS *Providence* (CLG-6). The accident took place in the Gulf of Tonkin shortly before a planned raid on North Vietnam's Haiphong Harbor.

With this critical operation about to occur the following day, Jacobs was tapped to take over as operations officer and complete the yet unfinished master plan to ensure close cooperation between the naval surface and air components. Jacobs skillfully accomplished the task, earning not only the praise of the Seventh Fleet senior staff but also being awarded the Meritorious Service Medal.

Following this three-month assignment, Jacobs found himself back at the Naval War College in Newport taking the Command and Staff senior course. Upon graduation, he was not only ready for command but he was a newly promoted commander and itching to go to sea. Rather than the destroyer he had envisioned, however, his new command would be a three-year-old destroyer escort, USS *Kirk*. "I was not at all disappointed," Jacobs emphasized. "*Kirk* was a first-rate fighting ship as capable as any destroyer."[17] And he was determined to accomplish any mission his man-of-war was called upon to perform.

Characteristically, that eagerness was tough to hide. During the change of command ceremony atop *Kirk*'s flight deck on August 29, 1974, the seated guests noted his impatience. As Cdr. Harold Burgess, the departing CO, barely completed reading his orders relinquishing command, Cdr. Paul Jacobs leaped to his feet to read his orders placing him in charge.

Kirk's new skipper began assessing his ship's condition and readiness even before the ceremonial pomp and giddiness had worn off the following day. He had already been informed that the ship was scheduled for WESTPAC (Western Pacific) deployment early the following March.

As with all the previous ships he had served in, Jacobs evaluated *Kirk*'s capabilities and learned her peculiarities. How would the ship perform with her single screw and rudder? He was used to destroyers with twin screws and twin rudders, which made them very maneuverable in most conditions. By going ahead one-third with one propeller and back one-third with the other, a vessel could turn in its own length without anyone ever touching the helm. In contrast, maneuvering a single-screw ship in close quarters was almost always a delicate balancing of helm and throttle—throwing the prop in forward or reverse while turning the wheel port or starboard. With an adverse wind and current, the process might resemble anything from a beautiful ballet to a badly fought boxing match. How the turning maneuver worked out depended on the ability of the ship's captain and the helmsman's skill.

Jacobs had already encountered much of this exotic equipment on board his new ship with the exception of the LAMPS (Light Airborne Multi-Purpose System) helicopter. He was already familiar with the ASROC (antisubmarine rocket) launcher capable of hurling nuclear-tipped depth charges toward a hostile submarine. Jacobs certainly noted but was not at all intimidated by the sheer sophistication of *Kirk*'s antisubmarine technology. As before, these advanced weapons were merely new challenges he would quickly master.

Getting to know his officers would be his other priority. As XO, Lt. Cdr. Dick McKenna would become Jacobs' trusted adviser and execute his decisions. Lt. Jerry Kolman, the ship's operations officer, had jurisdiction over the CIC and all the ship's electronic equipment and communications gear. Lt. Hugh Doyle, *Kirk*'s engineer officer, had responsibility for the ship's largest department, maintaining her main propulsion plant and all of *Kirk*'s other machinery. Lt. Garry Cassat, as weapons officer, was responsible for the ship's 5-inch gun, as well as her torpedoes and ASROC. Lt. Lou Arcuri, supply officer, saw to *Kirk*'s provisions, clothing needs, crew's pay, and whatever else was required to maintain a man-of-war. Ens. Bruce Davidson was both personnel officer and the ship's navigator.

Some time after taking command, the new captain remained on board after the workday to have dinner with several of his officers. After lively back-and-forth banter, he told them about his plan. "What are we gonna do, Skipper?"[18] "We're going down to clean the fire room," Jacobs casually asserted, noting earlier that those bilges were too grungy for his tastes.

In hindsight, he added, "I wanted to set a precedent that as long as I was in command, I wouldn't tolerate dirty bilges."[19] He also wanted to demonstrate to his subordinates that he wasn't afraid to get his hands dirty. The men met a few days later in their dirtiest work clothes, and for the next five hours, which stretched into the wee hours of the following morning, Jacobs and three of his officers scrubbed bilges until, as he remembered with a wry smile, "they were almost clean enough to eat off of."[20] With his engineer's eye, he noted and tagged each leak he encountered that required repair.

At the beginning of the next workday, he strolled into the chiefs' mess to have a cup of coffee with his chief petty officers, the men who really ran *Kirk*'s everyday operations either in port or at sea. On board *Kirk*, the division of "officer country" and "sailor country" did not exist. The ship was "Jacobs country" from her keel to the tallest antenna. BTC John Gornto was the first to speak: "Skipper, I understand you were in my bilges over the weekend." When it came to their areas of responsibility, chiefs could be very territorial.

"That's correct, Chief. I wouldn't be down there if those bilges were clean."[21] Jacobs' comment was duly noted. Within an hour, the entire crew was talking about the "bilge incident," and cleanup fever quickly spread like a virus throughout the ship. Sailors cleaned, painted, and polished anything and everything in sight. Each division now competed for the new CO's attention.

"'Captain, I want you to come to my spaces and see how clean they are.' It was as though someone had lit a fire under them," Jacobs said with a commander's pride in his voice.[22]

Kirk's new CO had inherited an efficient staff of officers and a well-trained and motivated crew. He was lucky. The Navy had been through some rough times in the past several years, reflecting what the civilian community was experiencing. The military services were not immune from the antiwar movement and the proliferation of drugs, which even found their way on board ships of the fleet, including *Kirk*. Even so, Jacobs' strong stand and his ability to handle the problem were also testaments to his leadership.

"We took a very strict stance on the drug thing," recalled Lt. Cdr. Dick McKenna, *Kirk*'s XO, "but, at the same time, redemption was also part of it."[23] The ship certainly had its share of disciplinary problems, but Jacobs' brand of justice meted out at captain's mast—whether strict or lenient—almost always seemed to elicit the right outcome.[24] The XO called to mind the most effective punishment the captain could wield: "You get thirty days restriction, you're reduced in rate, and we're gonna write your mother. Once word got around that we were writing mothers, that had its own impact."[25]

Social unrest being felt nationwide also manifested itself in racial polarization that erupted in 1972 on board two carriers—*Kitty Hawk* and *Constellation*. Prior to coming to *Kirk*, FN Bob Heym had been assigned to *Kitty Hawk* shortly after race riots had occurred on board that ship. "There was a lot of tension. Most of the snipes[26] carried a wrench wherever they went just in case they were attacked so they'd have something to defend themselves with."[27]

Heym considered his assignment to the destroyer escort a stroke of luck. The racial tensions he had experienced earlier were not evident on board the smaller ship. "From the beginning, the atmosphere on the *Kirk* was much more civil and the people more tightly knit. Before long, I knew I was working with a great bunch of guys."[28]

If success depended on trust, the new captain had already earned it with the men down in the engine room. Heym recalled that he didn't really expect much of a change after Jacobs took command:

> As snipes, we spent a lot of time down in the bilges and the engine room getting oily and dirty. Almost as soon as he came aboard, he somehow arranged for every one of us to get some coveralls to wear. That gesture resonated with every snipe on the ship. He actually knows we're down here! He won over everyone even before he had a chance to have much interaction with us. I was very good friends with a boiler technician named John Poole. John started referring to the captain as "Uncle Jake," so we all started calling him that. Somehow, word got back to him that he was being called "Uncle Jake" and it just tickled him. He always had a way of letting us know that he cared about us.[29]

The sailors who manned wooden warships in the early U.S. Navy grew up in coastal towns where seafaring was a tradition. Not so in the 1970s. *Kirk*'s sailors hailed from every part of the country and came from every ethnic tradition. The crew was truly an immigrant alloy poured from America's melting pot—Anglo, Eastern and Southern European, Hispanic, African American, Filipino, and Asian. Their names tell the story: Scott, McClellan, Doyle, Compiano, Swenson, Burinskas, Martinez, Dufrene, Soderborg, Lumaban, Ong.

Snapshots from *Kirk*'s 1975 WESTPAC cruise book provide a visual representation of those young men. In the 1960s and 1970s, with the nation torn by controversy over an unpopular war and political turmoil, hair was a statement—a badge of individuality tailored to the wearer's politics and musical tastes—conservative to radical, classical to acid rock. If their civilian counterparts ashore had the liberty to express their politics and individuality with their hairstyles, *Kirk*'s sailors found ways, within the confines of their military situation, to express their views. Chief of Naval Operations Adm. Elmo Zumwalt had, in fact, not only relaxed long-standing regulations regarding dress and appearance, but he eased restrictions on sideburns, mustaches, and beards.

At least to their new skipper—an individualist himself—appearances bore no apparent connection to a sailor's proficiency and dedication to doing his job and doing it well. Bearded and mustachioed, crewmen went about their business running their complex ship efficiently. They were constantly preparing USS *Kirk*—and themselves—for war. With his eye on their March 1975 deployment, Jacobs began honing their skills to a sharp edge.

Deployment was not automatic. *Kirk* first required certification that it was ready with a minimum of two qualified watch sections. Jacobs wanted three. To reach that goal, veteran sailors and newcomers alike needed refresher training for skills they already had acquired and familiarization with the latest technology. That instruction focused on the operation and maintenance of newly installed equipment and systems. A complex antisubmarine warship was constantly being upgraded with the latest communications, weapons, sonar, and radar technologies.

Kirk hummed with activity, and the tempo only increased throughout the fall and early winter months of 1974. If the ship took on the appearance of a floating classroom, her pier was often crowded with vehicles delivering supplies and vendors hawking sandwiches, snacks, and soft drinks from their mobile "roach coaches." Contractors came on board almost daily representing manufacturers of every supply product from an ice-making machine for *Kirk*'s galley to the radar antennas atop her superstructure. Their comings and goings also disrupted the training schedule.

These distractions were a constant irritation to the new CO to the extent that he hastily decided to move the ship to a mooring in San Diego Bay where he could train his crew free of the dockside chaos. Although this unorthodox action raised a few eyebrows, no one in authority could fault Jacobs for his decision—or for his results.

With all three watch sections finally qualified, *Kirk* headed out of San Diego on March 4, 1975, for her second WESTPAC deployment. The guided-missile destroyer USS *Towers* (DDG-9) steamed with her, and both warships steered a course for Pearl Harbor at a leisurely sixteen knots. About halfway to Hawaii, one of *Kirk*'s crewmen developed acute appendicitis, an emergency that forced the ship to divert north for a rendezvous with a fast combat support ship (AOE), a larger vessel having surgical capability. After transferring the patient, *Kirk* was now far behind *Towers*, a situation that offered Jacobs an opportunity to satisfy his impish competitive spirit while testing the crew's ability to pull off an all-hands exercise in deception.

Jacobs ordered flank speed, pushing *Kirk* to nearly twenty-nine knots in a dead calm sea while maintaining strict radio silence. Despite regulations that authorized *Kirk*'s LAMPS helicopter to fly only within a thirty-mile radius of the ship, Jacobs ordered his pilot to push that radius out sixty miles in order to locate *Towers*. When the guided-missile destroyer pulled into Pearl, *Kirk* had already been tied up for several hours. Paul Jacobs had pulled off his "sting exercise" with characteristic aplomb.

The ship remained in Pearl Harbor just long enough to top off fuel tanks and respond to a message designating her flagship of DESRON 23 for RIM-PAC (Rim of the Pacific) exercises. These drills were to take place in Hawaiian waters with military forces of several Asian nations. The maneuvers would further ready the ship for her WESTPAC deployment to Southeast Asian waters. Coming on board as commander of DESRON 23 was Capt. Donald "Pete" Roane and his staff. While on board, Roane would hold the title of commodore.

Following the successful RIMPAC exercises, which lasted about ten days, *Kirk* returned to Pearl Harbor to again fill her tanks. She was to escort the carrier USS *Hancock* (CVA-19) to the Philippines. *Hancock* had just off-loaded her air wing of fighter aircraft and taken on board a number of heavy transport helicopters. This action pointed to an impending evacuation of American personnel either from South Vietnam or Cambodia. Both nations, it seemed, were on the brink of collapse.

Until they reached the Philippines, *Kirk*'s crew members would see no letup in the pace of training. Junior officers saw duty on the bridge to qualify as officer of the deck (OOD) which would allow them to con the ship. This was done under the supervision of an experienced officer. Anyone who would find himself on the bridge as OOD would have to be as skillful in maneuvering the ship as the skipper himself—and that meant in all wind and sea conditions. With but a single screw, special skills were required.

"We'd pull ahead of the *Hancock*, put a buoy over the side, and [I'd] let my officers make approaches on that buoy," Jacobs said. "My whole day was focused on that crew, making sure that we had them trained not just on paper but really trained and [that] they knew how to respond without direction."[30] The captain would make his men practice until they could make the proper approach on any object. And that "object" might someday be an unlucky crewman who had made an "unscheduled departure" from the ship and ended up in "the drink."

To drill for that eventuality, Jacobs made a life-size dummy of foam covered with canvas and configured to look like himself with "CO" stenciled on the back. He would throw "Charlie Oscar" over the side followed by the shout of "Man overboard!" replayed through the ship's speakers. The idea was to maneuver *Kirk* upwind of the dummy, stop the ship, and pick up the "victim" without running him down or sucking him into the prop wash. Jacobs threw the dummy overboard whenever the fancy struck. Any time—day or night—crewmen might find themselves responding to "Man overboard!" until they got it right. Jacobs initiated this exercise at least once a day until his crew could retrieve a real victim in a matter of minutes. Just weeks away, that training would save the lives of two downed pilots.

The enlisted crew worked just as hard as the officers during the transit. Sailors were assigned four-hour watches. Bob Heym, who worked as a fireman in *Kirk*'s engine room, recalled the routine: "It was a long day if your watch began at 4 a.m. You'd work your watch, then you'd have your regular 8-hour workday, which ended at 4 p.m. Then you'd again assume your watch which finally ended at 8 p.m. We tended to rotate those watches about once every week and move through a cycle."[31]

In port, the sailors found the routine dull and uninspiring. "It was slow and you'd rather be on the beach," Heym remembered, but added, "[I] liked the daily routine of being under way. I liked the swaying rhythm of the ship, the constant sounds and vibrations of the operating machinery, and I liked being on the ocean."[32]

Life on board *Kirk* was not all standing watches, maintaining equipment, and trying to locate Charlie Oscar among the swells at midnight. Some crewmen had brought their guitars, saxes, trumpets, and drums on board, and Captain Jacobs encouraged them to join the ship's band. The sailor-musicians played at "steel beach picnics" on the flight deck or during tense and demanding underway replenishment operations. When *Kirk* drew alongside an oiler to take on fuel, the band stationed itself forward of the mack (mast and stack) where the action was to entertain the personnel.

"It was a lot of fun playing rock and roll music while we were rockin' and rollin' with a bigger ship right next to us," recounted Heym, himself a guitarist. "As we played, the most unreal echo would come back. Acoustically, it was an experience like no other. It all made for a lot of fun."[33]

And the music and picnics on the deck also seemed to make the work go faster. When the workday ended, the men could unwind with a spirited game of volleyball on the flight deck or by learning karate from RMC Lorenzo Gassaway, an accomplished black belt. After dark, those crew members not on watch could take in a movie on the mess deck or simply contemplate water foaming in the ship's wake.

As the daily underway rhythm became routine, Jacobs continued to nurture his relationship with the enlisted crew. He took particular interest in the non-rated sailors—the junior crew members without specialized training. These were the men at the very bottom of the ship's hierarchy who performed the menial tasks. Some had washed out of technical school. Others had been "busted" for bad behavior and would serve out their enlistments assisting in the galley, doing janitorial services, scrubbing bilges, and lubricating machinery. As "deck apes," they handled lines, chipped and painted, polished brass, and performed "other duties as assigned."

Jacobs saw each of these sailors as an untapped resource, an individual with the potential to "make something of himself." And, as captain, he would see to it that each sailor—rated or non-rated—would get that opportunity. At the time, Jacobs' sons were coming up through the Boy Scouts. "In fact, he used to bring the Boy Scouts to the ship on weekends to chip paint," recalled Dick McKenna. "And they loved it because we served pancakes on the mess decks. But that speaks to his interest in the growth of young people."[34]

Jacobs noted how successful one Boy Scout program had been in motivating scouts. He would borrow and modify the Boy Scouts' "personal growth agreement conference," which offered a roadmap for personal development. Every non-rated enlisted man on board *Kirk* would receive his own invitation to participate.

"About 6 in the evening, I'd bring the man into the wardroom along with his supervisors and the sailor's records," Jacobs said. "Also present were a few officers, including the XO, the ship's yeoman [secretary], and personnelman. I would then ask them, 'Tell me about yourself. What are you going to do with the next year of your life? Where are you going to be a year from now or five years from now?'"[35]

Heym remembered his own experience. He had been demoted from petty officer 3rd class to fireman for committing a serious infraction on board his previous ship. He was simply putting in his time in *Kirk*'s engine room until his enlistment was over.

> I had finished my workday and was on my way to the fantail to pass some time until it was my turn to go back on watch in the engine room. Out of the blue, I was summoned before the captain. Wondering what I had done that was so serious that I would be summoned to the wardroom, I was ushered in and told to sit down across the table from the captain. I felt more than a little relief at that, figuring that if I were there because of a mess-up, I would not have been greeted so cordially and told to sit down!

Heym continued, "Captain Jacobs had several folders on the table in front of him. There were several other officers in attendance, as well. He looked me straight in the eye and said something like: 'Fireman Heym, I really ought to kick your butt from one end of this ship to the other and back again.' That got my attention! Maybe I did mess up—big! Or maybe not. He probably would have told me what I did wrong by now if I had really screwed up. Thankfully, he didn't let me hang there wondering for too long."

Then Captain Jacobs proceeded, "I've been looking through your records. Did you know that you have scored higher on every test that you've taken in the Navy than any other man on this ship?" Heym shot back, "No, sir, I don't think that I've ever even thought about that."

The captain went on, "I have a problem. I have a man here—you—that appears capable of taking on a bigger role on my ship, but I can't put you into that role because you're just a fireman. I have too many firemen. What I need is another petty officer. I see that you were once a petty officer, so you're qualified to be a petty officer again. Did you know that since we're under way—and are in the war zone—that I have the authority to reinstate you to petty officer 3rd class?"

Heym responded, "Well, sir, I hadn't thought about that before, but it makes sense that you would." The captain then said, "If I were to reinstate you to petty officer 3rd class, what kind of petty officer would you be for me?" Heym thought for a moment and then replied with assurance, "I'd be as good as any you've got, sir." Jacobs smiled but countered, "I like that answer, sailor, but it's not that simple. I have enough 3rd class petty officers. What I really need is a good 2nd class petty officer, one that I can count on. If I was to reinstate you to 3rd class, would you agree to complete the course work for 2nd class in time to be eligible for promotion on the next cycle?"

Heym quickly said to himself, "I know that would give me less than a month to complete a course that is usually completed over a three-month period. My heart raced as I looked inside myself for answers. Can I do that? Yes, I can. If that's what it's going to take, I'll do it." Looking directly into the eyes of the resolute captain, Heym firmly replied, "Yes, sir, I will get my course work done and turn it in." "Good," Jacobs affirmed, "then we have a deal."

The captain wheeled around to one of his officers and spoke quietly to him, then turned back to Heym and said, "Okay, here's the way it will be. I am reinstating you to petty officer 3rd class, as of today, right now. I am having this reinstatement made retroactive to the date that you were demoted, which will give you the time in grade to be eligible for 2nd class on the next eligibility date. So you will also get back pay for the difference to make up for what you would have made if you would have never been busted. Of course you have to get your course work completed on time to be in the pool for promotion to 2nd class, which you agree to do, correct?"

"Yes, sir, I will do that." "Great! Congratulations, Petty Officer Heym." Heym recalled, "We shook hands, and I think I floated out of the room."[36]

Years later, the fireman-turned-petty-officer remembered, with affection, the man who gave him a second chance. "He approached all his duties with a level of joy," Heym keenly observed, "and it was easy as a sailor to enjoy working for a leader like that. His leadership style made you think you were part of a team doing something very important. What you did and the way you did it made a difference."[37]

Kirk and *Hancock* continued steaming westward at high speed toward a rendezvous with USS *Midway* (CVA-41) in the San Bernardino Strait for what turned out to be a dangerous late-night aircraft exchange. *Hancock's* remaining jets flew to Cubi Point Naval Air Station to make deck space available for more CH-46 and heavy-lift CH-53 transport helicopters currently on board *Midway*. Besides providing *Hancock* with escort protection, *Kirk* now had the critical role of "plane-guarding two aircraft carriers in the middle of the San Bernardino Strait going thirty knots with junks all over the place," Jacobs called to mind.[38] In the event of a mishap, the destroyer escort was to rescue downed air crewmen from the water.

Chief engineer Lt. Hugh Doyle remembered the operation as being "kind of hectic. It was night plane-guarding at very high speed, but it was an interesting professional training program for us because a lot of our young officers had never really operated at high speed behind a carrier."[39] The transfer of aircraft was in preparation for what appeared to be the evacuation of American personnel from Cambodia, a country now about to fall. What kind of action awaited *Kirk* and her crew could only be imagined. But their skipper had indeed done his very best to prepare them, and they were more than ready to show him and the Navy what they could do.

THREE

DUNKIRK IN REVERSE

THE HELICOPTER JUGGLING act, the operation that took place in the San Bernardino Strait in the Philippines, was barely over when *Hancock* and *Kirk* were on their way to Cambodia. Operation Eagle Pull, the evacuation of American personnel from Phnom Penh in early April 1975, was in motion. Although *Hancock*'s helicopters played a key role in that undertaking, *Kirk* saw little action. "The code name was 'eagle pull,' but there were so many delays and false starts that we began calling it 'turkey jerk,'" *Kirk*'s chief engineer, Hugh Doyle, remembered.[1]

Following that operation, *Hancock*, *Midway*, and *Kirk* were ordered to make a port call in Singapore. Crewmen would have an opportunity for some well-deserved liberty, while some of Doyle's engineering crew would perform routine maintenance on *Kirk*'s boilers.

On April 16 *Kirk* and her companion ships steamed into Singapore, but their time in port lasted only thirty-six hours. American sailors had hoped to luxuriate in hotel pools and enjoy Singapore's exotic nightlife for a few days. But they found their idyll abruptly cut short as U.S. Navy shore patrolmen fanned out across the city alerting men to return to their ships. COs had received the order for an "emergency under way." Their services were urgently needed off the coast of South Vietnam.

Within hours all *Kirk*'s sailors were back on board. Doyle and his men, however, faced their own emergency. Both boilers had been completely disassembled for cleaning, a difficult and time-consuming task, and parts and boiler pieces were scattered all over the fire room deck. "Suddenly we were put on a twenty-four-hour notice to get under way. My memory from the standpoint of the chief engineer is: 'Hey, you've got to put those boilers back together in twelve hours!' And then an hour later it was: 'You've got to have them back together in eight hours!'"[2] Despite the circumstances, the men went into high gear, reassembled one boiler, and had it back on line in time for *Kirk* to cast off and get moving.

Heading down the river at night and bucking a nine-knot current, the warship exited the mouth of the Singapore River and steamed north chasing *Hancock* and *Midway*, which, by now, were out of sight. Down in the fire room, Doyle's men were hard at work reassembling the other boiler.

The sea ahead was clogged with so much traffic that the helmsman had a tough job avoiding other vessels. "It was like being on the freeway with all the shipping," Captain Jacobs recalled, his problem-solving mind already seeking a solution to their dilemma.[3] Spotting a U.S.-flagged supertanker just ahead, he got on the radio and asked if any Maine Maritime graduates might be on board. The ship's XO responded that the chief engineer was a Maine Maritime man. When Jacobs spoke with him, he learned that the engineer had been one of his father's pupils.

Jacobs then made his big pitch to the tanker's chief engineer: "I don't want to keep dodging these junks while we head north. I'd like to pull in behind you and you crank that thing as fast as it will go. My max speed is about twenty-eight knots, and I need to get up off Saigon because it's about to fall."[4] The engineer answered affirmatively. *Kirk* could indeed haul in behind the supertanker, which by this time had increased its speed. "You could see the other ships move away as he made a path for us," Jacobs said. "He probably saved us an hour and a half in transit up there."[5]

Their destination was the South Vietnamese port of Vung Tau where a huge assemblage of ships, Task Force 76, had already gathered about twenty miles offshore. It was everything the Seventh Fleet could muster—seventeen amphibious ships, two aircraft carriers, fourteen escorts—mostly destroyers and destroyer escorts like *Kirk*—and eleven replenishment ships. Buttressing this close-in force, but working farther out to sea, was another group of ships under the command of Rear Adm. Robert Coogan. His flagship, USS *Enterprise*, was one of the two carriers comprising that second force. This second force was supposed to provide protection for the first group of ships. Rear Adm. Donald Whitmire was the amphibious force commander and was in overall charge of the evacuation. His flagship was USS *Blue Ridge* (LCC-19). The entire force numbered seventy-three ships.

What had been the "handwriting on the wall" was now reality. South Vietnam was about to fall, and U.S. intelligence feared the North Vietnamese could march into Saigon in another day—or in a matter of hours. Americans still in South Vietnam were ordered to get out: military advisers, CIA operatives, embassy personnel, and "sensitive" Vietnamese who had aided the United States during the long conflict. The initial plan was to use fixed-wing aircraft operating out of Tan Son Nhut Air Base, just north of Saigon. But with North Vietnamese troops on the outskirts of the city, and the airport's runways within range of enemy rockets and artillery, evacuation from that air base was now impossible.

Plan B, a helicopter evacuation known as Operation Frequent Wind, was about to begin. Heavy-lift transport CH-53 Sea Stallions and medium-lift CH-46 Sea Knights were to launch from carriers and amphibious ships, land at predesignated locations in and around Saigon, pick up their passengers, and head back out to their mother ships. After refueling, they would return to Saigon for more evacuees. This shuttle service was to continue until the helos completed the operation.

Kirk arrived on station off the port of Vung Tau on April 27 and was assigned an area to patrol. "It was like a huge parking lot so that we could steam back and forth at maybe five knots," recalled Lt. Bob Lemke. "Every ship was assigned an area to stay in because there were a lot of ships out there in a relatively small area."[6]

Kirk's mission was to provide surveillance, routine escort and patrol, naval gunfire support if required, and antiair and antisurface protection for the force. But the real fear was enemy aircraft. "Our job was to sit there and act as an antiaircraft asset," Doyle called to mind. "We were concerned that North Vietnamese jets, which were thought to be operating out of captured Tan Son Nhut and Bien Hoa air bases, would harass the evacuation fleet. So we were there as one of many cruiser-destroyer types to provide protection."[7]

Rumors of North Vietnamese missile-firing patrol torpedo (PT) boats in the area were also causing jitters. Lt. Cdr. Daniel Daly, the force defense officer on Rear Admiral Whitmire's staff, assigned each ship a role in the protection of all ships from threats from both air and sea.[8] "The threat I was most afraid of," Daly said, "was a hypothetical case in which a South Vietnamese pilot, flying a legitimate mission, would decide to defect while he was in the air and would attack us. We would not be able to recognize the threat he would pose until he fired upon us. There was no real solution except to let him take his best shot and then kill him before he took his second shot."[9]

The morning of April 29, 1975, dawned with intermittent rain squalls scudding across a broken overcast sky with visibility about a mile. It would have been a typical beginning to an ordinary day on the South China Sea were it not for the presence of so many gray-hulled ships of the U.S. Navy bobbing on the flat, leaden sea.

On board USS *Kirk* another morning routine was about to begin. A recording of reveille crackled over the ship's 1MC (public address system). Sailors not on watch rubbed the sleep from their eyes and went for the showers. Others pulled on their work uniforms—dungarees and cotton shirts that were perpetually clammy from tropical humidity—and headed to the galley for morning chow, a ritual that for some was the highlight of their day. The same procedure was also taking place in "officers' country."

If a sailor's life had its dreary repetitive duties, Navy fare was not one of them—a subject on which enlisted and officers could agree. If it wasn't haute cuisine, at least they could all chow down on plenty of eggs—fried or scrambled, French toast topped with a sweet amber-colored liquid masquerading as maple syrup, bacon, hash browns, toast, and jelly. The officers and enlisted men also had a modest selection of dry cereal in little boxes with serrations down the center for easy access. Breakfast chow was washed down with copious amounts of strong Navy coffee, milk, thin orange juice, or the ubiquitous and legendary "bug juice," a sugary, grape-flavored Kool-Aid-like beverage.

The enlisted mess and officers' wardroom had one point in common. Both were gathering places where men could discuss the day's events on board their encapsulated floating world. Above decks, the division chief or the division leading petty officer called morning muster, an age old Navy ritual: Who was present for duty and who would end up on the sick list? After reading the ship's "Plan of the Day," the men would then head for their appropriate stations and begin their duties. Every division was headed by a commissioned division officer. Back in the wardroom, conversation focused on what was happening or about to happen. A nation in its death throes less than a dozen miles away dominated their thoughts and words.

The previous night, April 28, the ship had been ordered to proceed only twelve miles away. The Frequent Wind evacuations were apparently about to begin. The move seemed logical based on what the men could see on the horizon. XO Dick McKenna clearly recollected the scene:

> After evening meal, I was in my cabin reading or signing the Plan of the Day when the officer of the deck or one of his assistants called me and said, "XO, you've got to come up and see this." When I got to the bridge, the watch, plus a goodly number of sailors that had come topside, were watching the sky in awe. We witnessed the most memorable show of lightning that I have ever seen. It was of the heat lightning variety, jumping from cloud to cloud in large

groups continuously. The show went on for hours unabated. There was no rain and I don't remember ever seeing the lightning strike land or sea. Considering that Saigon was about to fall, I consider it the most ominous and foreboding display of nature I ever expect to witness.[10]

Others in the fleet observing the same phenomenon thought they heard large detonations coming from inland. They attributed the light show to the final battle for Saigon. Doyle recounted seeing "tracers and huge explosions going off at Vung Tau, just twelve miles away."[11] On board USS *Cook* (DE-1083), *Kirk's* sister ship, the XO, Lt. Cdr. Ray Addicott, beheld a sea dotted by small boats. Several contract ships from the Military Sealift Command were taking refugees on board. "Some had come down the river on barges that were being towed. There were thousands of people," Addicott vividly recalled.[12]

Lt. Bob Lemke had already had his own experience the day before with *Kirk's* fuzzy radar screen and then observed, through the "big eyes" binoculars, hundreds of small boats heading out to sea. Jacobs was in the CIC looking at a radar scope. In utter amazement he gazed at the screen, overwhelmed by tiny images flowing together in a single blob. "There were so many contacts that the screen was becoming white as small boats were heading out to sea. It looked like Dunkirk in reverse."[13]

Marine and Air Force CH-53s and CH-46s thundered overhead as they moved toward Saigon. Operation Frequent Wind had begun. MMFN Kent Chipman was on deck talking about the impending operation with several of his shipmates. "Everybody was just standing around, anxious and wondering. It was very quiet and then, suddenly, the whole sky filled with helicopters. You could hear them coming—that *thump, thump, thump*—from miles and miles away."[14]

In CIC, OS2 James Bongaard saw them on his radar screen. "All of a sudden these dots come racing out . . . dots across the radar screen. They were too fast to even mark. What are these things? And we're calling the bridge asking for visuals and they say, 'We have helicopters coming in, swarms of them coming in waves.' It was just wild!"[15]

Back on *Cook* Addicott had gone to CIC to monitor the situation, and he heard one of the radar operators exclaim, "Wow, look at these contacts!" What the radioman saw, Addicott recounted, looked like "a swarm of bees on the radar scope. At first we thought they were small craft, but on closer look they were going too fast. I went topside on the bridge and the sky was just full of helicopters. It was an amazing sight."[16]

Doyle was similarly astounded, recalling, "All of a sudden we were looking around and there's one, then two, then eight, then twelve, then fifteen, then twenty-five. Pretty soon, they were all swarming out. It was totally unexpected."[17] "Unexpected" perhaps, but not surprising. Marine and Air Force helicopters, which were loaded up with evacuees from Saigon, then headed back out to sea to discharge their human cargoes, just like homing pigeons. Hundreds of VNAF UH-1 Hueys followed close behind, hoping to land on the same ships. It was a natural decision for many Vietnamese pilots.

Doyle saw the situation for what it was: "A pilot had a Huey fully loaded with fuel. His family is standing next to him, and out on the horizon he knows there are U.S. ships. It doesn't take a genius to put it all together and say, 'Kids! Get in the airplane. We're going!' We had no advance warning. They just started coming."[18]

As it turned out, the fear of remaining behind was very real. The night before, a South Vietnamese CH-47 Chinook helicopter, filled with women, children, and several elderly passengers, landed on USS *Blue Ridge*. Lt. Cdr. Daniel Daly noted that the pilot had not even radioed or requested permission to land. "He explained that the war was lost and had been told that the Viet Cong planned to cut off the hands and feet of all pilots and kill their families. Feeling he had nothing to lose and a lot to gain, he stole the helicopter and flew to his neighborhood."[19]

Just before 11 a.m. on April 29, *Kirk*'s CIC reported an inbound South Vietnamese helicopter, which then flew overhead and out of sight. The crew noted that all the Vietnamese helicopters thumped over the top of their relatively small ship looking for bigger targets to land on, hopefully just over the horizon. "From their altitude," Doyle realized, "they could probably see them—the *Blue Ridge*, the *Hancock*, and the *Midway*—and all the rest of those ships that were receiving the big helicopters."[20]

AW3 Don Cox noted each helicopter that passed over and wondered why none had attempted to land on their open flight deck.[21] Others, including Doyle, were also caught up in the drama and saw the possibilities. "We never anticipated a helicopter landing on us but we started talking about it," Chief Engineer Doyle recalled. "Wouldn't it be great to grab a helicopter? Wouldn't it be great to take part in this? The captain also seemed eager to take a trophy home, but we were getting frustrated because these helicopters kept flying right over the top of us in great numbers."[22]

Doyle added with astonishment, "You could look around and maybe one ninety-degree quadrant of the sky would have fifteen or twenty helicopters at various altitudes and various distances and all heading out to sea. The captain kept saying, 'Can't they see our flight deck? Can't they tell that there's something right here? Why don't they land on us?'"[23] Wishing for a trophy quickly turned into the act of acquiring one. SK1 Jeffrey Swan, who had learned rudimentary Vietnamese during an earlier tour in South Vietnam, was called to CIC. In an attempt to advertise *Kirk*'s hospitality, he began broadcasting on the air distress frequency: "Ship 1087. Land here!"

As this invitation was going out, another message had just been received from the surface squadron commander directing *Kirk* to leave her station and refuel. The captain and XO were not only puzzled by this bizarre message, but Jacobs was furious and enunciated his displeasure in pungent, sailorlike terms. What was the meaning of this foolish order? They had just refueled two days before, and the chief engineer had reported their fuel state at 87 percent. Pulling up stakes at this point would send them many miles out of the action that was sure to take place in their immediate neighborhood.

The captain would creatively defy the order by deflecting the directive. Captain Jacobs reported that the ship was then in the process of recovering aircraft. McKenna later recalled, however, that that particular recovery situation was "not quite the case at the time. We were definitely trolling for a helo, but none had yet obliged."[24] Despite this unwanted distraction, *Kirk* prepared for a possible landing. An alarm sounded followed by "Flight Quarters! Flight Quarters!" blaring from the 1MC.

Nineteen-year-old AN Gerald McClellan, assigned to *Kirk*'s LAMPS detachment, immediately hustled to the hangar and put on his safety gear: yellow flotation vest, goggles, and cranial (helmet and hearing protection). At the same time, the four-man fire crew took their stations on the flight deck armed with fire hoses. One wore a distinctive fire-resistant silver asbestos suit and hood. Two other airmen from the LAMPS detachment, AW3 Don Cox and AW3 Mike Washington, donned wetsuits and, with swim gear at hand, stood by as designated rescue swimmers in case one of the helicopters crashed while landing. "We were prepared to get into the water and help rescue any survivors on a moment's notice," Cox recalled with exuberance.[25] McClellan took his position, his back to the right of the hangar door and facing aft. Before him, in the middle of the flight deck, was a painted white circle with an "X" in the center, the appointed landing target.

Around 2 p.m., after nearly two hours of broadcasting an invitation, a South Vietnamese Huey finally turned inbound toward *Kirk* with its navigation lights turned on. As it slowed and approached the fantail, McClellan, the designated LSE (landing signalman enlisted), began motioning signals to the pilot. With his two arms extended, he beckoned the Huey toward the center of the flight deck. He then held his arms out parallel to the deck, the recognized gesture for a hover. With the helicopter just feet above the deck, the airman brought in his arms and crossed them, which was the sign to land. It was a textbook landing, and all who watched McClellan's skillful and fearless ballet breathed more easily. *Kirk* had her trophy.

The young signalman might have breathed his own sigh of relief, for only after the passengers and pilot emerged did he realize that this was a Vietnamese air force helicopter, not an American one. "For all I knew, they were American pilots," he later admitted.[26] Eight adults and four children stepped onto the flight deck from the crowded but seemingly brand-new helicopter.

"When I saw that some were armed," McClellan recalled, "I thought, what if one of these guys was a North Vietnamese? We didn't know who they were at that point. How could you know who was North Vietnamese and who was South Vietnamese?"[27] They were neither North Vietnamese nor poor refugees but VIPs. One passenger identified himself as the deputy chairman of the South Vietnamese joint chiefs of staff. Another was a two-star general. The other person of importance, a Buddhist monk, announced that he represented all Buddhists in the province surrounding Saigon. After surrendering all firearms, the refugees were escorted away from the flight deck.

Everyone present realized that this pristine aircraft, with its unblemished green paint job, was a high-ranking general's helicopter and indeed a trophy worth keeping. Crewmen dragged it to the forward port corner of the flight deck adjacent to the hangar. No sooner had they chocked and chained it down than the sky resonated with the distinctive *whump, whump, whump* of other Hueys smearing the overcast with their exhaust. The English-speaking pilot of the general's helicopter agreed to go to CIC to communicate with his countrymen in Vietnamese. His services were badly needed because by this time the sky was full of helicopters, many low on fuel and all desperate for a place to land.

Less than fifteen minutes after the general's helo had touched down, another Huey was inbound intending to land. McClellan gently waved him in. As the pilot shut down the engine, twelve people emerged: a Vietnamese air force lieutenant, his wife and children, and several other airmen. "There were as many people as they could jam on the helicopter," Doyle remembered with shock.[28] As they were relieved of their weapons and ushered from the flight deck, he looked up and saw three more helicopters stacked above.

"Oh my God! What have we done! What are we going to do now? You could see them at various levels all on short final waiting to land. So this was the momentous decision, which I believe was Captain Jacobs' alone. And it was a very quick one. I don't know what went through his mind, but I can imagine his concern looking up there and knowing that there were a dozen or more people on each of those helicopters. And he's looking at the lives of fifty people stacked up waiting for our single flight deck. He then said, 'Over the side!'"[29]

Several sailors quickly dropped the safety nets on the edges of the flight deck to prevent snagging a ditched bird and damaging the nets. Twenty or so other crewmen crowded around the second helicopter and began dragging and shoving the nearly 2.5-ton aircraft to the edge of the flight deck, inching it along until it tipped over and fell into the sea. "It didn't matter if you were enlisted or an officer. Everybody lent a hand, including the captain," Cox related with pride.[30]

Jettisoning the second helicopter and most of the others that followed was no small task. Unlike their LAMPS helo, which had wheels and rubber tires, Hueys had metal skids. Making matters worse was the nonskid surface on *Kirk*'s flight deck. "It was like sandpaper," Machinist's Mate Fireman Chipman pointed out. "The helicopters were very hard to move. It would take twenty or thirty guys. Everyone would grab hold of the helicopter and move it from side to side and kind of wiggle it until we got it over close to the edge of the ship. We'd keep wiggling it until the skids got off the side. The weight of the helicopter on the edge of the deck would break the skids, and it would just start nosing over. Everybody would then shove on the tail and it would flip over."[31]

The Hueys then floated for about fifteen seconds before submerging. Not a minute after helo number two toppled into the South China Sea, McClellan coaxed another on board. "It just barely had enough room to land without hitting the hangar," he recounted.[32] Instead of coming directly in from astern like the others, this helo came in crosswise from the starboard side. As it neared the flight deck in a hover, the Huey crabbed sideways. Its main forty-eight-foot-diameter rotor edged uncomfortably close to the "trophy" bird, whose tail boom extended outward onto the flight deck. But McClellan held his ground. The helo landed and the pilot cut the power.

Chipman, who was manning one of the fire hoses by the side of the hangar, watched in horror as the drooping rotor blades suddenly struck the tail boom of the general's helicopter. Everyone nearby ducked instinctively as debris flew in every direction. "There was an ungodly noise like three or four cars wrecking at one time. The noise was tremendous. I thought the guy waving him in was gonna be dead. I don't know how he got through that alive."[33] All who witnessed this near disaster marveled at McClellan's coolness under fire. He never budged from his position on the flight deck.

Captain Jacobs had seen enough and warned, "We can't have this. We're gonna have a huge accident!"[34] In response to the captain's fears, several crewmen quickly repositioned the trophy helo so that its damaged tail boom extended over the side of the ship to get it out of the way.

Ens. Craig Compiano, the ship's supply officer, noted the likelihood of a major catastrophe on board their ship if the landings continued: "These guys who were flying out there were supposedly untrained and we were afraid they would crash, causing huge fires and explosions. So we vacated the back end of the ship as much as possible and had the crew move forward away from the fantail as they tried to land."[35] Compiano's fears were justified. Most of the Vietnamese helicopter pilots had never been over blue water before or even beyond the sight of land. Few, if any, had ever attempted to land on a moving ship, much less upon a tiny flight deck. And that fact wasn't lost on *Kirk* crewmen who now watched the unfolding drama as desperation brought more helicopters their way.

Despite the danger, more overpacked helicopters, some "running on fumes," swarmed above the ship, each waiting for the previous aircraft to be cleared from the flight deck. One Huey circling overhead drew gasps from the men on deck. The doors had been removed and inside were as many as twenty people crammed tightly together in a vehicle designed for fewer than half that number. When it finally touched down, Chipman noted that four or five people had one finger grasping a single D-ring attached to the floor. As for the other passengers, he observed that "there was nothing to keep them from falling out except holding on to each other."[36]

The machinist's mate was also struck by the desperate looks on their faces and their state of mind. He lamented, "They lost their entire country, and the rug had been pulled out from under them. They had nowhere to go and didn't know where they were going. Most didn't even have a suitcase. But they were calm. There was no screaming and hollering, but there were very few smiles and no laughter."[37]

This scene repeated itself many more times in the next several hours as Airman McClellan waved more helos on board while his shipmates scrambled to clear the flight deck. Each Huey dumped over the side represented about a million dollars in value. Many went overboard with their "hoods" still up since mechanics from the air detachment did their best to salvage whatever equipment they could quickly unbolt from inside the aircraft, including electronics, radios, navigation equipment, and batteries. In one case, they removed a complete tail pylon assembly and hauled it into the hangar for spare parts.

Despite the frantic tempo, a definite order and procedure had developed. From the moment the first aircraft landed with armed passengers, security became top priority. Many crewmen at first felt uneasy and suspicious. As with

McClellan, who was uncertain about the nationality of the first arrivals, no one could be absolutely sure if all their "guests" were harmless refugees. Were Viet Cong or North Vietnamese infiltrators among them bent on commandeering the ship? Everyone had already heard chilling stories of murder and mayhem that had occurred on some of the overcrowded transports.

As each succeeding aircraft arrived and the passengers disembarked, men assigned to a security detail relieved them of their weapons, which included pistols, shotguns, automatic rifles, and even live grenades. Doyle remembered that almost every male adult had a gun. Hundreds of weapons ended up either stacked aft and placed under guard or in a locked room below—*Kirk*'s armory—which soon nearly overflowed with contraband. Even though the evacuees seemed to pose no threat, armed guards remained alert. Access to certain parts of the ship was curtailed, and, when necessary, refugees were assigned escorts. "At that point there was no way to know who was who," Compiano pointed out.[38] What was apparent was that these refugees were not peasants from the countryside. They were fairly well off and from South Vietnam's upper crust and military. Many of these first arrivals were families of some of the pilots.

A number of evacuees had fled with whatever wealth they could bring with them. Perhaps having anticipated the collapse of their nation for some time, some had converted their South Vietnamese piasters—paper currency—and other personal wealth into tiny gold bars. These bars were "no bigger than a Wrigley Spearmint gum stick," Doyle marveled. "Some even had hidden gold sewn into the folds of their garments."[39]

Supply Officer Compiano, who also acted as *Kirk*'s disbursing officer, was charged with confiscating the gold, which communally added up to a huge sum of money. He and an assistant collected not only the precious metal but also worthless piasters and other valuables, providing receipts to the owners. They then deposited all the refugees' worldly wealth in the ship's disbursing safe, to be returned to the owners when they eventually left the ship. The entire process was to avoid the possibility of theft and potential violence. "I don't recall the thinking that started the process," Compiano stated, "but certainly if the currency and gold were put away with a receipt, there could be no argument about how much they came on board with when they left."[40]

That initial unease quickly dissipated as the men of *Kirk* recognized the scope of the tragedy that had befallen the refugees. "You could tell they were scared," Cox poignantly brought to mind. "They were almost in shock as you looked at their faces. The children, of course, were crying and scared. The women were just following along and basically would do whatever was needed. The men were trying to protect their families. They were doing everything they could to try to survive."[41]

Doyle, among others, had already recognized that circumstances were converting their man-of-war into a humanitarian assistance ship. "Up to that point, our mission was antiair warfare. We were supposed to run a picket line back and forth prepared to defend against North Vietnamese aircraft that would try to intervene in the evacuation. We were concerned about small boats. So we were still thinking 'shooting.' How are we going to take out that boat or that aircraft? As soon as the first helicopter landed, however, everything changed. There were women and children on board. What do we do now? We very quickly jumped into gear."[42]

With anywhere from ten to twenty people on board each helicopter, the refugee population was growing rapidly. The ship's head was made available for their sanitary needs, and the mess crew was soon providing food and water on deck to the new arrivals. Very quickly, the Supply Department and the ship's master-at-arms set up a holding area forward of the hangar and aft of the mack on the 01-level (the deck above the main deck) and began taking a census. The refugees now had a place where they could rest and begin to recover from their recent ordeal. "There were all kinds of women, infants, and children, and the women were crying. It was a scene I'll never forget," sighed Doyle.[43]

Crewmen laid mats and blankets and set up lean-tos, canvas tarps, plastic sheeting, and awnings to shade them from a blazing sun and tropical rain. They also provided blankets and distributed hot food. Many sailors, their hearts softened by the sight of distraught mothers and babies, tried to ease their anguish by bringing refreshments and distracting young children. Simple acts of kindness and compassion, coupled with the improbable sight of young sailors tenderly holding babies, brought smiles and laughter to refugees who now faced an uncertain future.

FOUR

A RIDE OUT OF THE WAR

ROM FAR OFF, the *whump, whump, whump* of a helicopter grew louder, portending another emergency landing. But as the aircraft appeared, *Kirk*'s sailors grew apprehensive. This was not a Huey but a twin-rotor CH-47 Chinook, the largest helicopter in the South Vietnamese inventory designed for carrying cargo or many passengers and crew. *Kirk*'s flight deck could not accommodate this bird. The diameter of the rotor disk was so great that any attempt to land would result in disaster. Its rotors would hit the helicopters already stuffed alongside the hangar, or take out the hangar and the ship's radar mast and superstructure with great loss of life.

The Chinook's epic journey out to *Kirk* had begun that morning in one of Saigon's residential neighborhoods. Miki Nguyen, barely seven, was the son of a Vietnamese air force pilot, Major Ba Van Nguyen. The boy heard the chopper approach his grandmother's house where he and his family had sought refuge. Miki had grown up in the barracks playing with other military children and knew Hueys and Chinooks by their sounds. And he knew this was a Chinook.

The helicopter set down in a soccer field near the house, blowing dust and newspaper in all directions. "Chaos [was] pretty much everywhere right in the front yard," Miki said. "I remember my mom running around trying to get my brother and sister and myself. All my dad's younger brothers and sisters were standing around surprised, as everyone was, surprised to see my dad land the helicopter there and pop open the door. The copilot came out waving at us to get on the Chinook."[1]

The huge helicopter immediately drew a curious crowd, including several policemen. Not knowing their intent, the helo's gunner pointed his M60 machine gun menacingly in their direction. There was little time for decision making. Ba Nguyen and his wife, Nho, had two other children—another son, Mika, about three and a half, and a ten-month-old daughter, Mina. They had also adopted two older children, a sixteen-year-old girl and her older brother. "We knew that we were to grab our bag and get on that helicopter. This was our chance, our ride out of the war," Miki recounted with great enthusiasm.[2]

The urgency of the moment was evident as Nho begged her in-laws to come with them. This was their last opportunity to escape the doomed nation. But they refused. Ba Nguyen's mother would not leave her house and the land of her birth. Certainly the communists would not bother a woman in her sixties. She and the others would remain behind and take their chances.

"All hell broke loose," Miki would later remember his father saying. "It was the Wild West, and it was every man for himself. In this case, instead of you and your horse, you had you and your Chinook."[3] With wife and children safely on board, Ba throttled the engines to full power and lifted off, blowing the roof off a neighbor's house with the Chinook's downdraft. Later on, Ba would learn from family left behind that they had to pay for a replacement roof. As the helicopter punched through the low-hanging clouds, a red warning light flashed on the instrument panel indicating low fuel. Under normal conditions, the pilot would have sought a quick landing zone to refuel. But Ba knew that nothing in Saigon was now safe from the North Vietnamese and Viet Cong. He would seek refuge beyond the city.

Out his left window, Ba saw a Huey apparently headed for My Tho about forty-five miles southwest of Saigon. After trying to raise the other chopper on his radio without success, Ba fell in behind. Although now running on near empty, he landed the Chinook beside My Tho Lake. It was now about 11 a.m. They were safe—at least for the time being.

Ba took money his CO had given him the day before, and some his wife still had in her purse, and distributed the limited funds to his crew and their passengers. He instructed them to have some fun in My Tho for the last time and then return to the chopper. But he elected to remain on board the Chinook with his family. He again studied the map and realized that even My Tho was in danger. If the South Vietnamese government still existed, he thought, perhaps they could reach an island offshore and await further orders from Saigon. At the very least, an island refuge would buy some more time to decide what to do next.

Ba instructed one of the crew to buy food with their remaining pooled money. When the man returned a half hour later, he brought one hundred kilos of rice, ten kilos of sugar, some dried food, and pots, pans, and kettles to cook it in. After stowing the newly acquired food and gear, the crewman told Ba what he had heard in town. The Americans had demanded by radio that all South Vietnamese pilots should attempt to escape from South Vietnam without further delay. Ba mulled over this new information for a few moments then shook his head. "Why do we have to listen to the Americans? We should wait to hear news from the Saigon radio station and then we can play it by ear."[4]

By now it was about 1 p.m. and everyone had returned, including a crewman who purchased some fuel for the Chinook's engines. Then Ba suddenly remembered that a South Vietnamese general had given him several bottles of Napoleon brandy as a gift. Out it came from where he had stowed it and he poured some for his comrades. The significance was not lost on anyone. This would be the last party of the 237th Loi Thanh Air Squadron.

Yet even as they tried momentarily to eclipse their bleak situation with drink, a high-ranking officer from the Vietnamese army suddenly appeared in a jeep and asked Ba where he would go next. Ba told him they would remain in My Tho until he heard from Saigon. "My God!" the officer shouted. "There is no one there now. If you stay longer, the police here in My Tho will arrest you."[5]

Ba conferred with his crew. Should they try to reach the American fleet offshore or fly somewhere else? Like his mother and siblings who elected to remain behind that morning, several My Tho residents they had recently befriended were offered space on the commodious helicopter. But these locals decided to stay because the future just seemed too uncertain. Ba's crewmen agreed that flying out to sea and finding the American fleet was their last, best chance. Ba would not stop in Vung Tau for more fuel. Fighting had also erupted in that city. Ba shook hands and bid farewell to those who chose to stay and wished them luck. Back in the pilot's seat, he quickly took off and headed southeast.

"It was excitement in a lot of ways," remembered Miki, "not knowing what you were going to do in the next hour—let alone the next day. But I felt safe with my mom and dad. I know my mom would tell a different story being frightful for her children—her baby—holding her daughter in one hand and another very young son in her other arm. It was very frightful for her, but for a young six-and-a-half-year-old boy, it was a sense of adventure."[6]

Ba saw the green rice fields below and familiar winding rivers with small houses like the one he grew up in. It seemed these rice growers were cooking lunch; white smoke curled up around the houses. And all seemed peaceful. The war had not yet come to this pastoral setting. He could not stop the nostalgic flood of sweet childhood memories that now washed over him. The people in Ba's town were kind and honest. He knew the people below had no idea that he and his family were flying away to freedom.

In what seemed like a few moments, South Vietnam's coast receded behind them as they headed out over the South China Sea. This territory was new and alien for most Vietnamese pilots and Ba was no exception. He had never flown over open ocean before, at least not this far beyond visible land. He grew more concerned as the minutes ticked by. The Chinook had no life preservers on board, and if they were forced to ditch, everyone would drown. The copilot, Chu-Mai Nguyen, brought him back to reality: "Do you see the black smoke at 11 o'clock? I think that may be the American fleet." "Okay. We will keep flying in that direction," Ba responded. "I am sure the fleet must be near there."

Ba and his copilot desperately scanned the horizon for ships, but the cloud cover limited their visibility. Chu-Mai Nguyen then gestured toward the lower center of the windshield, "There! Can you see it?" "Oh, it looks like a boat," Ba responded, relief in his voice.[7] Their salvation was at 12 o'clock—straight ahead, and their life raft—USS *Kirk*. On the emergency guard frequency, he heard the steady chatter of English. U.S. Navy ships were communicating with other inbound aircraft.

Ba approached the ship and made a wide circle around the vessel while he tried to raise *Kirk* on the emergency guard frequency. "He made his first approach as if to land on the flight deck," Doyle, *Kirk*'s chief engineer, recounted. "He was much too big for the flight deck. It would have been catastrophic had he tried to land."[8] With his limited English, Ba nevertheless communicated the situation on the emergency guard frequency: "I have eleven passengers including crew, two women, and five children. My fuel state is critical. I must soon land or crash into the sea."[9]

As he descended, Ba realized just how small this vessel was and the folly of trying to land without his rotors smashing into the ship's superstructure and radio and radar antennas—and the ship's crew was also well aware of this imminent danger. Three sailors on the aft starboard side frantically waved him off. In his headset he now heard a voice in his own language: "No! You cannot land here! Other, larger ships—aircraft carriers—are just a few miles out. They can accommodate you."[10] Ba responded firmly, this time in his native tongue: "I have little fuel. I will not attempt to land but will approach the ship's stern and hover there. My passengers will jump to the deck from the copilot's door. I remind you. There are women and young children. Please help us!"[11]

As Ba came around for another low pass, *Kirk* crewmen saw anxious faces pressed against the helo's Plexiglas bubble portholes. Ba skillfully coaxed the helo transversely across *Kirk*'s fantail, cockpit port, and tail starboard, always mindful of his aircraft's rotors. He had to maintain enough height for them to clear the flight deck—just a few feet down to his right—yet get low enough to the fantail deck for the passengers to jump from the right door with minimal chance of serious injury. *Kirk*'s LAMPS detachment personnel admiringly noted the pilot's airmanship. He was not an amateur.

Lt. Cdr. Dick McKenna, *Kirk*'s XO, called for volunteers. Their task would be dangerous: Stand beneath this massive machine with its powerful downwash, trust its pilot to maintain his position, and then catch or break the passengers' fall as they jumped.

"McKenna was taking volunteers," remembered former machinist's mate fireman Kent Chipman. "Once we found out what we were doing, we were shocked and surprised, but we were still anxious to help with the big CH-47. When he first came in, he got too low, hit our lifelines, and bent a couple of poles over that hold the lifelines up. Well, that was fixin' to be a major accident, and he could have crashed and we would have lost everybody, including the sailors who were back there trying to help. They waved him off and he lifted off and came back down. The noise and the wind were so tremendous you couldn't hear. One guy was telling us, 'Okay, get ready!'"[12]

Below the howling rotor-induced hurricane, expectant sailors awaited the outcome. Nguyen gingerly worked his controls until he had the helo perpendicular to the ship's fantail, then eased it ever lower. "He was ten to twelve, maybe fifteen foot above the deck and that's when the door opened," Chipman excitedly called to mind. "You couldn't tell how many people were actually in it. I didn't know if it was crammed as full as the Hueys that had come out."[13]

Ba motioned for Chu-Mai Nguyen to open the copilot's right-hand door. Ba's wife, Nho, could clearly see sailors awaiting them on the deck below. With her daughter in her right hand and a bag containing her worldly possessions in the other, she hooked an arm on the ladder beside the door. When sailors on the deck below signaled for her to jump, she leaned out and let go of her infant daughter.

"As I looked up, I wasn't sure exactly what was going to happen," Chipman related. "Then all of a sudden here comes a human—a baby! There was no way I was gonna miss and let that person hit the deck. As I caught the baby, I shouted, 'I got him! I got him!'"[14] After catching Nho's daughter, having mistaken the child for a boy, he ran back to the passageway and handed the baby off to another sailor. He then returned just in time to catch Nho in his arms. "I wasn't a very big person at the time myself. I only weighed 130 pounds. She wasn't very big [so] I was able to catch her as well."[15]

Miki remembered looking out the Chinook's open door:

It was very noisy, very loud, very windy in there. To those of us without any headphones, it was thunderous. I think my mom may have jumped before me. As I got toward the edge of the door and looked down, I saw several crewmen, all of them with their hands raising up and stretching out. I held onto a rope with my left arm and eventually let go, hoping that the crewmen down there would catch me. They did and it was a happy moment. For me, stepping onto the deck of the USS *Kirk*—that was the first footstep to freedom. And it was very symbolic, the hands reaching out and grabbing all of us.[16]

On board the Chinook, Chu-Mai Nguyen removed his uniform, unfastened his seatbelt, and walked from the cockpit to the back of the aircraft for the last time checking to see that everyone else was safely off. Then flashing the okay sign, he silently acknowledged Ba as though to thank him. Seconds later the copilot, too, was safely on board *Kirk* and waving his hands. The heroic pilot was now alone, having off-loaded all his passengers, but the *Kirk* crew didn't know at that time that everyone had jumped out.

"We thought the helicopter was going to ditch with all the people aboard," Doyle recounted. "So I was preparing and others were organizing everyone and getting them into life jackets and life rings. We didn't have enough life rings so we took extra life jackets and tied lines around them to throw to people in the water. We really thought we were going to try to rescue some large number of people from the water, not knowing that they had already been safely taken aboard the ship."[17]

In the pilot's seat, Ba prepared to execute a maneuver he had never anticipated—ditching at sea. He flew about fifty yards off *Kirk*'s starboard aft quarter, then using the helicopter's cyclic—the control stick located between his knees—he eased the helo's six wheels a few feet above the water. He next turned on the cyclic control's "forced trim," thereby enabling him to maintain the huge aircraft in a stable hover while he removed his holstered pistol and struggled out of his flight suit. Having accomplished this task, Ba swung the striped emergency handle on the Chinook's left side door forward ninety degrees and the panel dropped into the sea.

It was now or never. He depressed the thumb button atop the cyclic, moved the cyclic to the far right, then released the button, locking the control in place. As the Chinook slipped down and right, Ba leaped into the water, struggling to thrust his body beneath the surface to escape the scythe-like rotor blades. Unwanted buoyancy forced him back to the surface. Just feet away and now in its death throes, the helicopter resembled a whining, angry beast as its still-spinning rotors exploded in a fury of hurtling shards.

Chipman remembered watching the drama from *Kirk's* deck: "The rotors went flying off. We were scared because we thought they might come back toward the ship. But the rotors actually went away from the ship. It sounded like a massive train wreck."[18] "You could hear this whistling," Doyle said. "It was the rotors of the helicopter disintegrating and flying all over the place."[19]

Lt. (jg) Don Swain of *Kirk's* LAMPS helicopter detachment witnessed the helo's demise in the South China Sea: "The aircraft had come apart with shrapnel flying everywhere. The first thing we saw was a bunch of red coming up inside the foam of the aircraft and everyone said, 'Oh, well, he's dead. That's too bad. He didn't make it out.' And then he popped up. The red we saw was hydraulic fluid."[20]

"Everyone became John Wayne at that point," recalled Doyle. "You couldn't stop these guys. They just ran out on the fantail and jumped over the side. We must have had five or six sailors in the water all swimming like crazy and dragging life jackets with them. Of course, we didn't realize that there was nobody left in the helicopter. They were all aboard the ship."[21]

AW3 Don Cox, trained as a rescue swimmer, saw this massive jump unfold. "Bodies of *Kirk* crewmen jumped fully clothed into the water. It was just raining people in an effort to save this little man floating in the water. Our motor whaleboat raced out to find him. I believe that before it was finished, eight of our crewmen were involved. I didn't even get into the water."[22]

By this time, the Chinook had turned "turtle" with smoky vapor rising from the wreckage as seawater quenched its hot engines. The helo remained afloat for about ten minutes in a huge pool of red hydraulic fluid. It reminded Texan Kent Chipman of "a dead armadillo lying on the side of the road, with all its four tires sticking up."[23] The motor whaleboat quickly returned to the ship with several dripping crewmen and Ba Nguyen wearing only a pair of flowered boxer shorts and a checked shirt, an unlikely "uniform" for USS *Kirk's* latest hero.

Despite the happy outcome—no deaths and no serious injuries—the crew had no time for celebration. More helicopters were heading their way. It seemed that Airman McClellan would not get a break. By late afternoon, at least five more helicopters had landed on *Kirk's* deck. One more had been spared and tucked next to the hangar, its tail boom swung safely outboard.

Daylight began to fade around 4:15 p.m., and *Kirk's* Grimes light was turned on so an inbound helicopter could locate the ship. Fifteen minutes later, the aircraft was safely on deck, unloaded, and pushed over the side. The crew then got an unexpected forty-five-minute breather before yet another Huey requested permission to land. It touched down at 5:20 p.m., and after the passengers disembarked the pilot asked to be refueled. It seemed he had been unable to get his family out. Before it had left Vietnam, one of the passengers had boarded thinking the helo was headed for the Mekong Delta only to find herself now on board *Kirk*. She also wanted to go back. Captain Jacobs tried to talk her out of it, but, as McKenna remembered, "in the end she left on board the returning helo, which we refueled and sent on its way. We later learned that the pilot found his family and returned to one of the helo carriers."[24]

At 8 p.m. the ship was in for another round of "Huey madness." Two more helicopters were headed for *Kirk's* flight deck, with four more circling overhead. By this time all available lights had been turned on, bathing the ship and, more important, her flight deck in bright light. At 8:03 p.m. helo 1 was on deck. As its refugees ran from the open door, the ditching dance began again in earnest. Helo 1 went over the side at 8:09. At 8:10 p.m helo 2 was safely on deck. Four minutes later, it followed its predecessor into the South China Sea to make room for helo 3, which landed at 8:17. After unloading, it hit the water in time for helo 4 to land six minutes later. At 8:38 p.m. it was over the side.

Helo 5 was on deck at 8:41 p.m., followed by helo 6 at 8:53. Twenty-two minutes later, a very exhausted crew managed to drag it and themselves to the edge of the flight deck. Like the others before, it would end up littering the ocean floor. It seemed that even late-night darkness would not deter those so desperate to escape from their homeland.

Five minutes before midnight, one more helo landed on deck, an aircraft bearing the blue-and-silver paint scheme of an Air America Huey, owned and operated by the CIA. For now, at least, it would remain on deck where it had landed as the twelfth and last helicopter to find refuge on board *Kirk* that day.

FIVE

LAST GUNSHIP FROM SAIGON

COBRA PILOT CAPT. John Bowman was assigned to Marine Heavy Helicopter Squadron 462 (HMH-462), which was embarked on board USS *Okinawa* (LPH-3). The squadron's mission was to provide armed escort of transport helicopters—CH-53 Sea Stallions and CH-46 Sea Knights—whose intended assignment was the evacuation of Saigon. For days *Okinawa*, as with other vessels in Task Force 76, had been at the ready. The amphibious assault ship, cruising just a few miles off the South Vietnamese coast, awaited orders to launch aircraft for the evacuation. Bowman and other members of his squadron were up at 3 a.m. several mornings in a row pre-flighting their aircraft and standing by for the evacuation order, but each day it was the same situation. It was not yet time.

On April 29 the men were up early, as in previous days, but again, the operation was postponed. Around noon, as Bowman was standing in line in the officers' mess for lunch, he heard the announcement over *Okinawa*'s 1MC. Operation Frequent Wind was a go and crews were to man their aircraft immediately.

The midday launch posed a host of problems. The earliest the helos could arrive in Saigon was late afternoon with little time to execute the mission before darkness closed in. And because the evacuation mission was unrehearsed, men and machines would now confront many unforeseen problems. *Okinawa* was only one of several aircraft carriers and amphibious assault ships that would launch aircraft that day. "The whole business of the evacuation was extremely complicated because there were many different flight decks, lots of helicopters, and, of course, troops were spread all around who needed to get in to provide security," Bowman remembered.[1]

The operation began with the launch of a maximum number of empty helicopters. This "practice" launch would enable central control to determine how many of these transport helos it could handle at one time. The helos then landed on board their respective ships to refuel. The transports took on troops and then launched for the mission. To avoid aircraft trickling into the city two and three at a time, central control determined that at least fifteen helicopters should make the initial landings. Evacuees had been ordered to assemble at one of two landing zones (LZs): Tan Son Nhut Airport, also referred to as the Defense Attaché Office (DAO) compound because the DAO offices were adjacent to the airport, or the U.S. embassy. No one anticipated the magnet that the embassy would become both for evacuees and thousands of panicked Vietnamese clamoring to escape the city. Heartbreaking images showed desperate people attempting to scramble over the embassy's wall and Marines turning them back at gunpoint.

Nevertheless, during the earliest stages of the operation, several companies of Marines landed at Tan Son Nhut and set up a defensive perimeter. Vietnamese had already begun arriving by the thousands, overwhelming American personnel who were directing the evacuation. Marginal weather added to the chaos. Heavy overcast and a low ceiling aggravated by multiple fires on the ground, some from burning buildings, required a number of helicopters to fly on instruments.

"The city had been under fire for some time so Saigon was ablaze when we got there," Bowman related, "and there were people on the ground shooting at us."[2] The situation grew more tense as evening came and the light began to fade.

Captain Bowman and his copilot, 1st Lt. David Androskaut, were ordered not to land their aircraft but instead fly cover for the transport helicopters in and out of the DAO compound LZ. Their AH-1J Cobra gunship was well equipped for suppressing ground fire and deterring any trigger-happy North Vietnamese soldier or Viet Cong threatening the evacuation. Adapted from the Bell UH-1 Huey, the Cobra was slimmer than its parent, had two engines, and carried ample firepower with four 2.75-inch folding-fin aerial rocket pods and a 20-mm, three-barreled Gatling gun. The two-man crew sat one behind the other, copilot in front and pilot slightly above and behind him, beneath an elongated canopy that maximized visibility.

With approaching darkness and a smoky haze obscuring the DAO compound LZ, visibility was quickly decreasing. The communications situation was also marginal. A lone Air Force C-130 flying at a higher altitude provided an airborne command and control center, which relayed messages to and from the fleet at sea. But balky radios, heavy message traffic, helicopters flying in all directions, and the proximity of the enemy all added to the confusion.

In an effort to improve the odds, the Cobras broke off from the escort mission with several gunships flying over the DAO compound and other gunships patrolling above the embassy. Thus situated, the Cobras now acted as airborne beacons or pathfinders that helped vector in the inbound transport helicopters. For their crews—most of whom had never seen combat before—finding a landing zone in a large, darkened city in chaos was daunting.

Bowman and Androskaut maintained their position over the DAO compound, scanning the ground for enemy activity while sending out messages on their UHF radio—their primary communications. As they transmitted, the pilot or copilot of an incoming helo transport selected the automatic direction finding (ADF) feature on his radio. The radio's bearing needle then pointed toward the source of the transmission. "You'd come up on the assigned frequency and talk to the guy," Bowman said. "And then I'd give him a long count: 1, 2, 3, 4, 5, 6, 7, 8, 9, 10. During that count, the pilot would get a fix as to where I was. That's how we'd help get the transport helicopters into the landing zone."[3]

In addition to the radio aid and despite the combat environment, the Cobra pilots turned on their running lights and searchlights to help the transport helos find the DAO compound LZ. With a Cobra leading them, three CH-53s would approach the LZ. Just as they were about to land, the gunship would then break off. Its job now was to protect the helos and not allow any inbound aircraft into the LZ until those on the ground were loaded and ready to lift.

Bowman knew that thousands of terrified people filled the streets below. He realized if his Cobra took enemy fire, shooting back would most likely cause civilian casualties. With their running lights on and at minimum airspeed to conserve precious fuel until the next section of Cobras arrived to relieve them, their gunship was a target almost too tempting to pass up. "We just sat up there, smiled, and hoped," Bowman vividly called to mind.[4] Their goal was to stay as long as possible both to reassure their comrades still on the ground as well as to deter the enemy from attacking the DAO compound or firing at incoming or outgoing helicopters.

Bowman and Androskaut flew two round-trips to *Okinawa* before refueling for a final sortie into Saigon. This time their aircraft and another Cobra were to cover the embassy. Unlike the DAO compound where three helos could land at a time, the embassy's very limited space enabled just one helo to land. Only a single CH-46 Sea Knight or Huey could set down on the roof or a single CH-53 Sea Stallion or CH-46 in the embassy's courtyard.

Around 11 p.m. the section of Cobras covering the DAO compound ran low on fuel and headed home, leaving the compound swarming with hundreds of Vietnamese still waiting to board inbound transport helicopters. Apprised of the dire situation, Bowman keyed his radio mike and informed his wingman that despite orders to cover the embassy, he was breaking section integrity and heading to the DAO compound. "You stay here and take over. I'm going over there to run the Tan Son Nhut–DAO compound," he informed his wingman.[5] It was just after 11 p.m. on April 29.

Both gunships were getting low on fuel, but neither pilot knew what had transpired many rungs above them in the chain of command. Authority at the highest level—President Gerald Ford—had terminated the evacuation, and no more flights would be arriving. Low on fuel but confident his relief was on the way, Bowman's wingman abandoned the embassy and headed back to the ship. Bowman and Androskaut were now patrolling the airspace over Tan Son Nhut alone, oblivious that replacement gunships had not and would not be launched. "We still had about a hundred Marines on the ground, with the NVA just a few blocks away," said Bowman. "And there were disgruntled South Vietnamese army troops in and about the area."[6]

Very low on fuel, Bowman now had to make a critical decision. But just then his radio crackled with news that several sections of CH-53s were inbound. He and his copilot decided that despite their critical fuel state, they would remain on station to cover the evacuation of those Marines still on the ground. "We were not leaving before they got in to extract those men," Bowman emphasized. "We were not going to leave Marines unprotected during the final phase of the DAO evacuation."[7]

The two aviators watched the last Marines board the helos, saw the ramps go up, and then get airborne. "We did a low flyby just to let the NVA know we were still there," Bowman clearly remembered. "Then we covered their rear quadrant or six o'clock position and followed them out to the ocean."[8] That Cobra was the last gunship out of Saigon.

The short flight to the South China Sea was anything but routine. Even though they were safe from ground fire, Bowman and Androskaut had few visual references to aid their journey. Visibility was nil and they had to depend on their instruments. Although the ground was still obscured by clouds, thirty miles from Saigon Bowman radioed "feet wet," indicating they had probably crossed the coast. USS *Okinawa* was somewhere out in that sea of darkness, but Bowman could not get a bearing with his TACAN (tactical air navigation system). Either the ship wasn't transmitting the necessary signal or the Cobra's receiver was malfunctioning. Nevertheless, *Okinawa* radioed a vector and instructed them to fly a heading that would lead them home.

The Cobra's fuel gauge didn't ease Bowman's anxiety. He radioed the ship that he was at minimal fuel and needed to be directed to any ship that might have a flight deck. Although still on instruments, Bowman was now able to discern a clear sky above, but he was confused by the little white lights near what he thought was the horizon. Were they stars or lights on the ocean's surface? "They looked just about the same as a mast light on a ship down below," he thought.[9] They pressed on searching for their mother ship. All they could do now was fly at a landing pattern altitude and maintain the vector course *Okinawa* had assigned them.

About five miles from the ship, the Cobra's TACAN finally locked on, indicating they were right on track. Bowman suddenly observed a light below illuminating the gray funnel of what appeared to be a U.S. Navy ship. Was it *Okinawa*? No. It was too small, a frigate perhaps. USS *Kirk* happened to be right in line with *Okinawa*'s TACAN. It wasn't Bowman's ship but it had a flight deck that might offer emergency sanctuary to a Cobra nearly out of fuel. A low pass across the vessel's transom confirmed a flight deck, but one that was already occupied by a parked UH-1 Huey. For the Cobra's exhausted two-man crew, all good options had just run out.

On board *Kirk*, the day's intense level of activity had every member of the crew high on adrenaline. Even off-duty crewmen found it impossible to sleep. *Kirk*'s chief engineer, Hugh Doyle, saw that everyone "was really 'hopped up,' almost like being drunk."[10]

At 11:45 p.m. Ens. Bruce Davidson arrived on the bridge and after a brief exchange regarding *Kirk*'s position, he relieved Doyle as OOD for the 11:45 p.m.–3:45 a.m. watch. About five minutes past midnight, a low-flying helicopter approached the ship, its running lights plainly visible. EWC J. F. Willoughby, chief electronics warfare technician, commented to Davidson that it looked like an aircraft in distress. Doyle, who was standing just outside the bridge, recalled that the helo "came very close up our starboard side, heading for our flight deck as if he were going to land."[11]

The aircraft hovered over the flight deck like a dragonfly approaching a cattail when just as suddenly the pilot aborted the landing and flew up *Kirk*'s port side. Then making a right turn and crossing the bow, the aircraft headed off to starboard. Doyle yelled in to Davidson that he thought the helo was losing its engine. Then all was silent. The chief engineer instinctively ran back into the pilothouse, picked up the microphone, and shouted, "Helo in the water! Helo in the water!"[12]

"I flew over the *Kirk*," Bowman said, "and then, starved of fuel, both engines wound down."[13] Flying over water at night with no definitive horizon was naturally disorienting, so the two-man Cobra crew was still flying on instruments. As one and then the other engine flamed out, Bowman did what every Marine helicopter pilot was trained to do in such an emergency: He initiated an instrument autorotation. He dipped the nose slightly then lowered the collective control, which increased the spin rate of the rotor, noticeably decreasing their descent. When the radar altimeter told him they were seventy-five feet above the water, he pulled the stick back and began pulling the collective up to slow the descent even further.

Bowman's skills paid off. All forward momentum ceased and the Cobra settled gently into the ocean, its rotor still spinning. He quickly applied the rotor brake to prevent the blades from tearing into the water with potentially catastrophic results. The aircraft then rolled over to the right, leaving the copilot's canopy door on the upside. Androskaut could then leave the aircraft without having to open the canopy against water resistance. He tumbled out without difficulty but Bowman struggled to unbuckle himself. As the aircraft began settling deeper in the water on its side, he found himself hanging in the straps and unable to find his lap buckle. Ceramic body armor, worn over his flight suit and survival vest, somehow was preventing him from locating the buckle, which had worked its way up his chest.

For a brief instant the moon popped into view illuminating a desperate scene. Water was already coming in over the cockpit canopy and the gunship was sinking rapidly. Bowman frantically struggled to find the lap buckle a second time, again without success. Fortunately he had not blown the Cobra's explosive canopy when the helo hit the water because an air pocket inside the intact canopy bought him more time to locate the buckle, which he found on the third attempt. But now Bowman was trapped in the aircraft, which was already several feet beneath the surface.

"I took a big deep breath, reached up, and activated the escape handle. The canopy exploded, collapsed, and water came crashing in. I tried very carefully to ease my way out of the aircraft. I was maybe fifteen or twenty feet down. It was dark and I wasn't sure which way to swim. I felt the aircraft go one way so I figured I'd try the other way."[14] Even though he was now free of the helicopter, which suddenly disappeared, his body armor, survival vest, and other gear were dragging him down despite the fact that his life preserver had already inflated.

"I looked up and as the moon came out again, I saw my copilot's feet treading water about twenty feet above me. I guess I was halfway towards the surface when I thought, 'Why are you still carrying your body armor with you?' I finally pulled it off and was able to get to the surface a lot more quickly."[15] Bowman suddenly popped into view, and Androskaut was so relieved to see his comrade alive that he punched him in the arm with sheer delight. "The only injury I sustained was him banging on my arm because he was so happy," Bowman happily recalled.[16]

Just as he retrieved several signal pen flares from his survival vest to fire and turn on his strobe light, Androskaut told Bowman that something had just brushed against his leg. "I really didn't need to hear that, knowing there were some really big fish out there."[17] It wasn't a shark. The copilot's left knee board had drifted down against his ankle. Bowman managed to fire two signal pen flares into the sky, but they were unnecessary. Help was on the way.

On *Kirk*'s bridge Davidson continued where Doyle had left off. "Plane in the water! Plane in the water! Starboard side! Captain to the bridge!" he shouted into the mike.[18] But the skipper's services were not needed. Jacobs had instructed his officers well with his frequent and unannounced man-overboard drills. Acting instinctively, Davidson had already ordered searchlights turned on and had pointed the ship at full throttle toward the downed helo. Less than ten minutes after Bowman and Androskaut ditched their Cobra, *Kirk*'s motor whaleboat had plucked the two swimmers from the water.

Jacobs welcomed his dripping but grateful guests with some medicinal brandy liberated from sick bay. While their flight suits were being laundered, he ordered steaks from the galley for the two Marines.

After breakfast later that morning, Lt. Rick Sautter, the officer in charge of *Kirk*'s LAMPS detachment, offered to ferry both men to their ship. Ironically, Sautter would pilot the Air America Huey to take Bowman and Androskaut back to *Okinawa*. That helicopter, recovered close to midnight the day before and now tied down on *Kirk*'s flight deck, had been the one that had prevented their emergency landing. "They got it cranked up nicely and put us safely aboard the *Okinawa*," Bowman stated. "I guess the naval tradition is that when you retrieve aviators, the ship that finds you gets some ice cream. [The *Kirk*] got five gallons of strawberry ice cream to pay for our return."[19]

SIX

ARMITAGE

A T CHOW THAT Wednesday morning, April 30, *Kirk*'s crew was still marveling over the midnight rescue of the Marine pilots. Now they had something else to buzz about. The officers, who had already been up on deck and returned to the wardroom to refill coffee mugs, excitedly told their shipmates what they were seeing. It seemed a repeat of the morning before, but instead of dozens of small boats heading out to sea, hundreds of vessels were now fleeing South Vietnam.

When chief engineer Lt. Hugh Doyle finished breakfast, he went topside to see what the commotion was all about. "I thought I was going to see ten or twelve fishing boats. I went out on deck and saw ten or twelve HUNDRED fishing boats! I could hardly see the water, there were so many fishing boats.¹ By this time, *Kirk* had been detached from her station a few miles from the beach and was now directed to transfer her onboard refugees to one of the larger evacuation ships. Doyle noted that many of the "junk-type boats" were flying South Vietnamese flags and "going as fast as they could go."²

One evacuation ship, which had already taken on board hundreds of refugees, reminded the chief engineer of a candy bar laid on a summer sidewalk and just crawling with ants. *Kirk*'s XO, Dick McKenna, found it "spooky to arrive in the vicinity of the chartered ships of the Military Sealift Command and find them chockablock with refugees who had fled in this manner from Saigon, Vung Tau, and who knows where else."³ Moreover, this second wave seemed different from the "sophisticated" military personnel and urban families who had arrived on board *Kirk* on helicopters just twenty-four hours earlier. "The helo people were relatively calm," Doyle noted. "The Vietnamese fishermen and peasants who were coming out in these boats, on the other hand, were just in a frenzy."⁴ *Kirk* had received orders not to rescue any of the new boat refugees but instead stand by and protect the freighters as they loaded the evacuees on board.

About half past noon *Kirk* rendezvoused with SS *Green Port*, a freighter contracted by the U.S. government. *Green Port* was now familiar with consolidating refugees picked up by other ships in the task force. In a driving tropical rain, a landing craft from USS *Durham* conducted the transfer of *Kirk*'s 157 refugees. It was an emotional departure. Doyle recalled that as the landing craft "pulled away from the *Kirk*, everybody in the boat got up and gave us a round of applause, just whistling, clapping, applauding, and waving. I don't think they wanted to leave. It was really touching, and I don't usually get touched like that."[5]

For now, at least, *Kirk* was without refugees. The afternoon saw some more helicopter activity, but nothing like the crazed events of the previous day. Flying the Air America helo that had landed the night before, Lt. Rick Sautter, officer in charge of *Kirk*'s LAMPS helicopter detachment, and copilot Lt.(jg) Scott Steele lifted off around 5:30 p.m. and headed for USS *Okinawa* to return Capt. John Bowman and 1st Lt. David Androskaut, the two rescued Marine pilots, to their home ship.

At 5:50 p.m. another South Vietnamese Huey landed, and its passengers were soon on their way to USS *Okinawa* via motor whaleboat. This relatively new aircraft was another "keeper," but where to put it? The flight deck was not a candidate. It had to remain clear for future emergency landings. Lt. Rick Sautter had a solution. He and his designated copilot for this flight, Lt. (jg) Scott Olin, would fly the bird off the flight deck and then re-land on the ship's fantail, a narrow deck not designed for accommodating a helicopter. No one doubted that Sautter was a crack pilot, having demonstrated his airmanship many times before. But this maneuver was a particularly dangerous operation, and a slight misjudgment of just a foot could translate into a catastrophe.

"We all held our breath," McKenna recounted, "as the bird settled with the rotors within two to three feet of the flight deck edge. They had flown with such cool confidence in their own ability and the judgment of the flight deck officer that it looked like a piece of cake."[6] The crew spent the rest of the afternoon and evening re-stowing gear, landing and jettisoning two more South Vietnamese Hueys, and getting ready for whatever additional emergencies might come their way.

At 9:30 that night, after receiving a cryptic message—via secure voice radio—from Rear Adm. Donald Whitmire, the commander of Task Force 76, *Kirk* dispatched its motor whaleboat to the Joint Task Force flagship, USS *Blue Ridge*. The assignment was to pick up a mysterious civilian passenger. "When a CO gets a message from the Seventh Fleet [that the commander] himself would like to speak to you, come alongside, it gets your attention," Jacobs coolly remarked. "So I thought maybe we had done something wrong, not realizing that we were being picked for a special mission."[7]

McKenna and the other officers were naturally curious at this new development, especially after seeing whom their motor whaleboat had retrieved. "We observed a stocky gentleman in a sports coat and tie in the party," McKenna remembered, the XO noting that the circumstances seemed quite incongruous. "Here we are in the South China Sea with the bulkheads sweating with humidity, and all in short-sleeved shirts, Bermuda shorts, and sweltering."[8] "Stocky" might have seemed an understatement to others present who noted that the blazer could scarcely contain the man's barrel chest.

McKenna escorted the stranger to the wardroom where he identified himself as Richard Armitage. When Jacobs arrived moments later, Armitage explained that he was a special agent from the Department of Defense. After some preliminary conversation, Jacobs moved the meeting to his cabin. Armitage, Jacobs, and McKenna were then joined by Lt. Jerry Kolman, *Kirk's* operations officer, and Capt. Pete Roane, who was riding the warship as Destroyer Squadron 23's commander, making him the ranking officer present with the title of commodore. Noting that Armitage was packing a .45 pistol, Roane remarked that he was not accustomed to having armed civilians coming on board his ship in the dead of night. Armitage responded in a gruff voice, "I'm not used to coming aboard armed in the dead of night but I've got a job to do. I work for the secretary of defense."[9]

As Armitage began outlining *Kirk's* new mission, the officers grew increasingly uneasy. For these officers, only two civilians were in their chain of command—Secretary of the Navy J. William Middendorf and Secretary of Defense James R. Schlesinger. Yet Armitage already seemed to have taken charge. He briefly recounted how he had been in Vietnam with a mandate to save or destroy as much sensitive material and technology as possible. That knowledge could not fall into North Vietnamese hands. But the speed of South Vietnam's collapse had altered his plans and shortened the timetable. Although Armitage believed that most of the Vietnamese army had already surrendered, the Vietnamese navy was a different story. He explained that senior South Vietnamese naval officers had no intention of surrendering their ships.

Armitage next outlined the plan for rescuing what remained of that navy. Traveling alone and at night to mask her intentions, *Kirk* was to rendezvous with the remaining South Vietnamese ships at Con Son Island, more than one hundred miles southwest of Vung Tau. Armitage would then transfer to the South Vietnamese flagship, *Tran Nhat Duat* (HQ-3). Once on board, he and Vice Admiral Chung Tan Cang, chief of naval operations (CNO) of the Vietnamese navy, would supervise the escape to the Philippines. *Kirk's* officers listened with increasing apprehension. Jacobs pointed out that returning to South Vietnam unescorted would put his ship in danger of air attack since North Vietnamese fighters now controlled nearby air bases. Did Armitage realize that the destroyer escort was well equipped to fight submarines, but with its single 5-inch gun, the ship was virtually defenseless against hostile aircraft?

Armitage nodded. He understood the risks, having once been a destroyer officer stationed off the South Vietnamese coast. But then he emphasized that the gamble was worth taking. If they didn't carry out the plan, the ships could not be saved, and in the worse case scenario, their personnel would most likely be slaughtered. Although Armitage made a compelling argument, Jacobs shot back that no written orders existed for conducting this operation. At the very least, he insisted on calling *Blue Ridge* to verify the plan. The commander of the Seventh Fleet quickly assured Jacobs—via secure voice radio— that Armitage indeed spoke for the secretary of defense and that the plan had been endorsed by Rear Admiral Whitmire. Jacobs returned, adjourned the meeting, and immediately ordered a new course set for Con Son Island. The next chapter of USS *Kirk's* adventure was about to begin.

Who was this mystery man who was now calling the shots? Richard Lee Armitage was barely thirty years old the night he stepped on board *Kirk* and took charge. As a member of the Naval Academy class of 1967, he had set his sights on a Navy career. The fledgling officer drew his first shipboard deployment as a damage control assistant on board the destroyer USS *Buck* (DD-761) stationed off the Vietnamese coast, providing naval gunfire support to forces ashore. But the assignment offered few challenges, and Armitage, eager to get into the fight, volunteered for shore duty as an adviser to the Vietnamese navy.

Certainly anyone who met Armitage, then or since, could not fail to notice his natural talents. "He was a person with a very unusual combination of abilities," recalled retired Navy captain James Kelly, a close associate of Armitage during and after Vietnam. "He was a physical bear of a man. Later on in Iran, I roomed with Rich and he would begin the day with four hundred push-ups and three hundred sit-ups."[10]

Retired Air Force colonel Lawrence Ropka remembered his first impression. On an early morning road trip to Vung Tau to assess the naval situation in that port, Ropka was riding in the rear seat. "In the pre-dawn darkness, I could hardly see who was in the front seat but for the Vietnamese driver and a guy beside him with a neck the size of my waist."[11] If Armitage appeared forceful in a physical way, the combination of skills James Kelly noticed was very apparent. Armitage's gift for the Vietnamese language was one such aptitude. Kelly related, "He had the ability to pick up languages the way a piano player might play by ear."[12]

Admiral Tan Lam, who was the South Vietnamese CNO until just weeks before the fall of Saigon and who was replaced by Vice Admiral Cang, insisted that Armitage's fluency was so complete that he could switch from a southern to a northern dialect with the snap of a finger. A close South Vietnamese naval associate, Captain Kiem Do, noted that Armitage could tell a joke in the language and have his Vietnamese comrades rolling on the floor. Americans and Vietnamese who served with him assert that native speakers, who conversed with Armitage over the phone and then met him for the first time, were astounded to learn that he was not Vietnamese.

After just a few weeks of formal language training, Armitage apparently honed his skills "on the street" working with South Vietnamese naval units in the Mekong Delta and teaching ambush techniques. For a time Armitage was a counterinsurgency instructor at the Naval Amphibious school at Coronado, California, specializing in ambush and interrogation. Armitage served a second Vietnam tour in 1971, and a third tour a year later as an adviser to another ambush team working along the coast. Rumors abounded that he was also a participant in the controversial Phoenix Program. But Armitage has never confirmed involvement in this counterinsurgency program.

But what made Armitage stand out among his contemporaries was another skill even more extraordinary than his physical strength and grasp of the Vietnamese language. He absorbed the culture and ended up loving the Vietnamese as a people. That quality gave him a special relationship with the South Vietnamese military. In the Delta, he lived with his South Vietnamese counterparts, ate their food, donned the black pajamas they often wore, slept on the ground, and freely shared their hardships.

"It was something that transcended rank," asserted Kelly. "Senior people knew and respected him. Ordinary Vietnamese knew and respected him. He was 'Mr. Tran Van Phu,' 'Phu' being a synonym in Vietnamese for 'Rich.'"[13] Immediately after the war, when Armitage was involved in helping resolve the huge refugee problem, he frequently visited the many camps set up to accommodate those now without a country. "I saw this among the refugees later on," Kelly recalled. "He'd walk through there like the Pied Piper. All of a sudden this comet's tail of young and old would start following him along just wondering what he was going to do and say. It was a very special gift."[14]

Following the signing of the Paris Peace Accords in January 1973, Armitage suddenly resigned from the Navy. He reasoned, "I resigned my commission because I didn't agree with the tenets of the Paris ceasefire. I've likened it to getting a woman pregnant and then running out on her. I thought we had gotten the Vietnamese into this endeavor and we were running out on them."[15] Despite this parting with the service he loved, the Vietnam pull was just too strong. Because of his language skills and familiarity with the country, the DAO in Saigon asked him to become the naval, Marine, and airborne operations adviser working out of that city.

If Armitage had won over the hearts and minds of the Vietnamese, he also earned the unqualified trust of his new superiors who found him to be an indispensable resource. He knew the Vietnamese military and had its complete confidence. Moreover, he realized, as no other American did, how the war was going, how military assistance was being utilized, and what further support was actually needed. When Erich von Marbod, principal deputy assistant secretary of defense, organized a task force and sent Cdr. James Kelly to Vietnam to gather intelligence, Kelly recalled that "almost everyone said the guy I should see was out there in Vietnam, a GS-12 operations specialist whose name was Rich Armitage. He knew much more than anybody else."[16]

Others on von Marbod's staff who went to Vietnam in those post–Paris Peace Accords days were equally impressed. Ropka recounted, "[I] learned more about what was going on with the Vietnamese Navy and the U.S. Navy than I had learned any time previously. [Armitage] had it lock, stock, and barrel—chapter and verse. I was amazed."[17] As the North Vietnamese began deploying more forces into South Vietnam in clear violation of the Peace Accords, von Marbod made frequent trips to Vietnam to make his own assessments. He, too, called on Armitage.

Von Marbod related,

The information we got was very useful to us as bureaucrats in the Pentagon. When I went to Vietnam, I relied on Armitage for advice because I didn't know the situation on the ground that well. I never got the impression that he was trying to manage perceptions in a way that was favorable to the Vietnamese, the Americans, or himself. He always came across as very sincere, very pragmatic, and very honest. He would explain to me what had been, what was, and what was likely to happen. And if you were under fire with him, which we sometimes were in the Delta, he wouldn't be distracted. He was a very natural and very brave person. I learned then and later that he had bureaucratic courage. Some guys would not say something because it wasn't the right thing to say or do. But Armitage would tell it like it was."[18]

Armitage left Vietnam and joined von Marbod's staff at the Pentagon. He worked for a time in that team position until he resigned and went back to his home in San Diego in the fall of 1974. On March 10, 1975, the North Vietnamese launched their climactic offensive of the war with an estimated 100,000 troops, Soviet-supplied artillery, armored vehicles, and surface-to-air missiles. Armitage returned to South Vietnam on his own to see for himself what needed to be done. "I found that the situation was deteriorating much more quickly than was evident in our newspapers," he said.[19]

The second week of April, an unsympathetic U.S. Congress rejected the Ford administration's request for an additional $722 million in emergency aid for the beleaguered nation. South Vietnam was doomed. When Armitage returned to San Diego, he called von Marbod's Pentagon office to relate the urgency of the situation. James Kelly picked up the phone and listened to Armitage's story.

"I checked with Erich and his first words were, 'Tell Armitage to get his ass here to Washington,'" Kelly related, clearly remembering von Marbod's words. "The following morning, Rich appeared after having flown all night. By early afternoon, we executed papers to make him a secretary of defense consultant."[20] On April 24, Ropka, von Marbod, and Armitage arrived in South Vietnam with the intention of trying to save whatever people and equipment they could. Von Marbod and Ropka would focus on getting American helicopters and fixed-wing aircraft out.

Armitage, who was familiar with the naval end of the situation, remembered his specific orders: "Effect the destruction or removal of sensitive equipment, as well as major naval assets to prevent them from falling into the hands of the North Vietnamese—in short, to break, destroy, and deny things to the North Vietnamese."[21] Armitage's first agenda item was to call his old friend, Captain Kiem Do, deputy chief of staff for operations. The two had served together earlier in the war and had developed a good rapport.

Do recalled,

Armitage said that he wanted to meet with me at my office, and he came about half an hour later. He told me that the situation was desperate, and that the United States did not want to let the fleet fall into the hands of the communists if they took over the country. I agreed with him but didn't dare to make any suggestions because politically it was too risky for an officer to talk about running away with the fleet without the authorization of the higher-ups. So we made a plan and I told him that this plan was very, very dangerous. I just cannot do it on paper. So nothing was written down. However, I did report it to Admiral Cang.[22]

The "E-Plan," as Do referred to the evacuation strategy, was complex: Of the Vietnamese navy's forty-five largest seagoing vessels, only thirty or so were deemed in good enough condition to make the escape. Presumably those ships would afford space to tens of thousands of refugees despite the fact that neither Do nor Armitage mentioned refugees in their discussions. A wink and a nod on that score would suffice for now. Do then suggested that the ships could rendezvous at Con Son Island, 115 miles southwest of Vung Tau. The island was close to the Mekong Delta where the Mekong River enters the sea. This proximity would allow the smaller boats of the "brown water navy" to get out and join the fleet. The target date for the evacuation was May 2 or 3, the most likely dates for the final enemy assault on Saigon.

Vice Admiral Cang consented to the evacuation plan but told Do that this strategy might cost both of them their heads if this scheme were made public. Sending ships out of the country could be perceived as an act of treason both by the existing government and by the communists if they took control. The choices were limited: Evacuate the ships or surrender them to the enemy. Armitage returned to Naval Headquarters in Saigon on April 27, this time accompanied by von Marbod, who quickly surmised that the naval staff knew very little of the setbacks suffered by the Vietnamese army and air force.

"When Armitage and I met with them [Vietnamese naval staff], they weren't talking about fleeing or bugging out," remembered von Marbod.[23] As far as he could tell, these officers were still at war and ready to fight. Before the meeting ended, details of the E-Plan were in place. Armitage then headed for the air base at Bien Hoa, northeast of Saigon, to carry out his mission of destruction.

He arrived at the abandoned Bien Hoa Air Base on Monday morning, April 28, accompanied by several U.S. Air Force master sergeants to help with his task. Armitage's first priority was to remove sensitive equipment from the Precision Measurements Laboratory housed on the base. He was unaware that advance units of the North Vietnamese army were already in the vicinity. Only a few days before these units had fought and defeated the Vietnamese army's 18th Division at Xuan Loc in the last desperate battle of the war.

Armitage had been noting that through the course of the day stragglers from the Vietnamese army were showing up. "They figured their best chance for survival was to stick with us," Armitage recounted.[24] He made a deal with these army troops. If they'd help him destroy the items on his checklist, he promised to get them out of their predicament.[25]

Von Marbod was aware of the deteriorating military situation. He knew the position of North Vietnamese forces on Route 1, but a situation far more ominous was developing. Radio intercepts of the enemy's intentions made von Marbod nervous. The North Vietnamese knew Americans were at the Bien Hoa base, and one message, in particular, was quite specific: "We have the enemy surrounded and will kill them all." Von Marbod related, "After getting that intercept, I called Armitage and said, 'We've gotta pull you out of there.'"[26]

The response was characteristically Armitage. According to von Marbod, Armitage began arguing. Von Marbod told him in no uncertain terms, "I know some things you don't know. Get your ass out of there!"[27] But Armitage continued to heatedly disagree over when he should evacuate the base. He told von Marbod that he did not want to come out. His job wasn't done and he had some people on the base who depended on him, and he added that he had promised to help them. But Armitage finally relented, and von Marbod radioed that he would send a helicopter right away to evacuate him and his comrades.

"No!" Armitage warned, "If you send a helicopter, we all won't be able to get on because we've got about thirty South Vietnamese, and they're not gonna let us get on a helo and leave them. They'll shoot us!"[28] Von Marbod quickly located a CIA contractor, Bird Air, a company that sent a Thailand-based C-130. At about 4:45 p.m. the plane touched down on the runway and spun around. Armitage, the two Air Force personnel, and the thirty Vietnamese made a run for the transport under fire. Like a chase scene from a Hollywood movie, one of the Vietnamese rode his motorcycle up the ramp and catapulted over the handlebars into the aircraft. "We all got on board and the plane made a corkscrew takeoff," Armitage said, vividly remembering several bullets that tore harmlessly through the C-130's aluminum skin. "I looked back down at the airfield and saw it just overrun with North Vietnamese."[29]

He and his fellow escapees landed at Tan Son Nhut Air Base a few minutes before 6 o'clock in the evening. They had touched ground just in time to witness a bombing attack by four A-37s. These attack aircraft had been captured by the North Vietnamese the previous month. Unscathed by this latest attack, Armitage and his boss, von Marbod, reunited at the DAO headquarters at Tan Son Nhut to compare notes. One such note was a transcript of the intercept that had marked Armitage for death, and von Marbod pointed out just how close his colleague had come.

Armitage now realized they had no time to waste. He commandeered a jeep and drove to the Vietnamese Navy Headquarters where he spent the night. He hoped to update Captain Kiem Do on the urgency of the situation. Early the following morning, a barrage of 122-mm rockets impacted the DAO compound. In a second-floor bedroom, von Marbod leaped out of bed just as one rocket hit the base of a concrete blast wall below. The force of the explosion leveled his bedroom wall.

Von Marbod clearly recalled those terrifying moments: "[The explosion] screwed up my hearing a little bit. It blew the clock off the wall, which had stopped at 4:05."[30] The rockets also took the lives of Darwin Judge and Charles McMahon. These two Marines were the last Americans to be killed in action in Vietnam.

Armitage awoke to the sound of distant explosions. He then went outside the South Vietnamese naval headquarters building where he had spent the night. "[I] saw a Vietnamese Air Force C-130 which had been hit by a missile," he recollected. "It was trailing smoke, circling down, and crashing. I decided I better go to Tan Son Nhut [air base] and find out what was going on. I took four Vietnamese and the five of us drove through Saigon and it was just chaos. There was looting and drinking and raping and shooting going on throughout the city."[31]

When he arrived at DAO headquarters, which was still taking incoming rockets and artillery fire, von Marbod was waiting for him at the operations center. He told Armitage that he was trying to get a helo out to *Blue Ridge* to confer with Rear Admiral Whitmire and that Armitage was to accompany him. Armitage, the subordinate, shook his head. "He wanted to be with his people—the [South Vietnamese] navy," von Marbod recollected. "I pressed him for quite a time that morning, but he insisted that he needed to go to Navy Headquarters and to give them an update. Then he left and did not go with me to *Blue Ridge* on my helicopter."[32]

Armitage next drove back downtown to Navy Headquarters where he called Captain Do and other officials of the Vietnamese navy. He stated,

"Rather than leaving on the 3rd or 4th of May, which was our original plan, we had to effect the evacuation that evening, the 29th. I would meet them at Con Son Island. They were to take all capital ships that they didn't destroy at Con Son Island and put as many people as possible on board. Captain Kiem [Do] and I had talked about some things we might do, but nothing about the plan had been discussed with the U.S. forces at all. So, in effect, he and I were winging it. I then went back to Tan Son Nhut, got a helo out to the *Blue Ridge*, and started to effect the plan."

It was easier said than done "to effect the plan." When his helo landed on *Blue Ridge*'s flight deck, Armitage appeared to be just another fleeing American civilian in filthy clothes and wearing a .45 in a shoulder holster. Armitage recounted, "I looked around as I came off the helo and saw the flag lieutenant. I said, 'Lieutenant, this is going to be hard to believe but I'm on a mission from the secretary of defense and I need to see Admiral Whitmire.'"[33] The young officer was immediately skeptical. Who was this imposing yet scruffy man with a three-day growth of beard demanding to speak to the Task Force commander? Surely he must have some means of identification.

Armitage told the officer, "I have no wallet, no passport, no identification. Please tell the admiral that I dressed under his picture in the athletic facilities at the Naval Academy every day for three years."[34] Armitage relied on this "secret handshake" to grant him access. Whitmire had been a football great both at the University of Alabama and the Naval Academy, and his portrait hung prominently in the Naval Academy's athletic facility.

The lieutenant returned fifteen minutes later and escorted him to Rear Admiral Whitmire's quarters. Armitage introduced himself and told him that he, too, was a Naval Academy graduate, that he now worked for the secretary of defense, and was on a mission from the secretary of defense. Armitage told the admiral that he could send a message back to the Pentagon to confirm it. The reply from the secretary of defense's staff was not long in coming. Armitage said, "It confirmed not only that I was who I said I was but that Admiral Whitmire and his colleagues were to follow my instructions."[35]

Why Whitmire chose *Kirk* among all the other vessels in Task Force 76 to carry out this hazardous mission is still a matter of conjecture. It was probably because Capt. Pete Roane was riding that ship as the commander of

Destroyer Squadron 23, making him the most senior officer on the scene. But *Kirk* had displayed an exemplary record and the fact that Capt. Paul Jacobs had a reputation as a can-do commanding officer certainly did not hurt.

When the big man in the borrowed blazer and tie boarded USS *Kirk* after 9 p.m. on Tuesday night, April 29, 1975, the thirty-year-old civilian, with extraordinary skills and determination, had the full confidence of the commander of Task Force 76.

SEVEN

VESSELS OF OPPORTUNITY

J OSEPH PHAM, OR Pham Xuan Vinh, as he was known in Vietnam, had roots in what would be called North Vietnam as of the 1954 partition. His earliest memories as a six-year-old boy were of war. The youngster's countrymen had fought Japanese invaders, and then the communist Viet Minh battled the French when World War II ended. To escape the strife, Pham's family had been forced to leave his birthplace of Hanoi and resettle in their ancestral village. But even in this rural village, no one was safe.

"There was a lot of fighting between the Vietnamese communists and the French—and I was in the middle of it. Sometimes we had to hide to avoid the bullets and the crossfire, and take refuge in the rice paddies where it was cold."[1]

The Phams then returned to Hanoi in 1952. Two years later, during the great migration south, most refugees left on board U.S. Navy ships. But Pham, his mother, father, and three siblings arrived in Saigon on board a French military plane to begin a new life free of communist dictatorship. Despite experiencing some discrimination, the family adjusted well to life in South Vietnam. As devout Catholics, they had imported and sold religious objects in Hanoi. In Saigon they opened a retail shop dealing in sacred icons. Pham went to elementary school, high school, and then to college at the University of Saigon where he majored in literature.

As the ruling Diem family consolidated its power in the late 1950s, Pham began to witness the social and political unrest. This everyday turmoil in Saigon lasted until November 1963 when a coup overthrew President Ngo Dinh Diem. The former president and his brother Ngo Dinh Nhu were assassinated. With each succeeding government, the situation in South Vietnam grew more unstable as one coup followed another.

"The Viet Cong had been waging guerrilla war against the South Vietnamese government since 1959 and it kept getting worse," Pham recalled. "In [March] 1965, the Marines landed in Danang to help the South Vietnamese government."[2] Shortly thereafter, Pham entered the Army of the Republic of Vietnam (ARVN) as a draftee. Prior to that, his fluency in English, learned as a youth, earned him a job as a medical interpreter funded by the U.S. Agency for International Development (USAID). Now in the army, he worked with military medical teams in several provinces, including Pleiku near the headquarters of the U.S. Army's 4th Infantry Division. The proximity to Americans enabled him to further hone his English language skills.

When Pham reported for military duty, he entered the ARVN's officer candidate school at the Thu Duc Military Academy. Following graduation, he drew an assignment in Binh Duong Province, a hotbed of Viet Cong (VC) activity. Because of his English fluency, he worked with American military advisers as an interpreter. In 1971, Pham attended the Defense Language Institute at Lackland Air Force Base in Texas to learn training methodology. By that time he was married with a son.

When he returned home to Saigon, American involvement in the war was already winding down and the South Vietnamese would soon be responsible for their own security. As the North Vietnamese launched their full-scale offensive in March 1975, the situation in the northern part of South Vietnam quickly deteriorated. "My brother-in-law was an army officer in the artillery unit in Pleiku and was in the chaotic migration from Pleiku to the south," Pham said. "On his way, he was captured by the Viet Cong and spent several years in a labor camp."[3]

With enemy pressure on the capital becoming critical, Pham's family situation became equally precarious. His wife was pregnant with their second child, but he was unable to attend to her because his unit, which was stationed near Tan Son Nhut, was on high alert almost every day. For two days, April 28–29, the VC attacked Tan Son Nhut Air Base and its airport with rockets and mortars causing many casualties. "My unit was very close to the air base. Even though the violence kept unfolding before our eyes, we had to defend our compound as best we could. People were fearful of the collapse of Saigon at any time because so much chaos was going on in the city. I felt the collapse would come sooner rather than later. And I was in the middle of it."[4]

Pham witnessed the attack close up and clearly saw the firestorm at the edge of his compound on April 28. The following morning his wife called to announce that she was having contractions. He used that excuse to obtain permission to leave the compound and go home. But even though his house was just a few miles away, the trip on his motor scooter seemed an eternity. Refugees, abandoned vehicles, and military equipment clogged the roads. Soldiers discarded their uniforms to pose as civilians. Many brandished their handguns.

Worried that his wife was about to give birth, Pham arrived home to discover that it was a false alarm; she wouldn't deliver her child until a few weeks later. Nevertheless, he knew time was running out. Rumors flew that the Americans would evacuate some of the people who had worked with them, and he certainly fit that description. Pham and his wife hurriedly packed a few belongings. Holding their young son on their laps on the tiny scooter, they rode to one of the rumored rendezvous locations. But no one else showed up and the promised helicopters never came.

"We ended up going from one rendezvous site to another. In some places there were many people."[5] At soccer fields or open spaces, Pham found desperate refugees trying to claw their way on board the few available aircraft. Fearing for his wife and young child's safety, he gave up the helicopter option and reluctantly went home.

The following day, April 30, all three Phams remounted the scooter and made their way to the waterfront. They spotted a merchant ship tied up alongside the river, but it was so crowded they could not board. Remembering that the naval yard was nearby, they rushed there and found another ship. Even though it was already crammed with refugees, Pham and his wife and son were among the last to clamber on board as the gangway was hauled up.

Their getaway ship was *Lam Giang* (HQ-402), a World War II–era U.S. Navy assault landing craft (LSM). Just over 200 feet in length, the ship normally had a complement of fifty sailors and five officers. Wedged on deck and in every available space were an estimated five thousand men, women, and children.

Although *Lam Giang* was a vessel of opportunity for the escapees, the choice was anything but ideal. The landing craft had been in the yard for a major overhaul and repair of bow doors that refused to close all the way. But that essential repair job had not been completed. Stationary at the pier, watertight integrity of the doors did not seem that important. But once under way, water poured into the ship at an alarming rate, as the refugees soon witnessed.

Manila lines were cast off but electrical cables, which still ran across the decks and onto the pier, held the ship fast. Someone found a fire axe and sweating men and boys began swinging wildly, severing the cables and showering the deck with sparks and the accompanying ozone smell of errant high-voltage electricity.

Finally free of the pier, *Lam Giang* swung stern-first completely out of control, blue smoke rasping from one of its two operating diesel engines. The steering motor didn't work, and a generator functioned only intermittently. Above the din, a voice of authority—whom the refugees took for an officer— ordered several men to manhandle the steering wheel. "Turn the wheel twenty degrees to the left!" yelled the unseen commander. Even as the men complied and the bow swung crazily in the opposite direction, the voice out of nowhere then shouted, "Forty degrees to the right!"[6]

The weathered wooden spokes peeled skin from fingers and knuckles as a dozen volunteers fought to bring the ship around bow-first. When the steerers collapsed from exhaustion, other men took their places. The effort was pointless as the Saigon River's stubborn current and an uncooperative breeze kept *Lam Giang* pointing stern-first downriver.

When the vessel approached the bank nearest the end of Tu Do Street, one of Saigon's chief thoroughfares, a North Vietnamese army (NVA) tank turret traversed its movement. Someone suggested they hoist a white cloth as if to offer surrender, and then maybe the NVA wouldn't shoot. A soldier removed his white T-shirt and hung it from the stern. The sight of the gray landing craft and its surrender flag traveling backward downstream must have seemed bizarre, yet comical, to the communist tank crew. They held their fire as *Lam Giang* slowly disappeared from view around a curve.

Approaching dusk now favored the hard-luck vessel, but several small fishing boats and rafts came alongside with more refugees to add to the ship's perilously high population. Then a widening river finally enabled the ship to come around, bow first. Even though her speed was barely five knots, her forward motion scooped in water through the damaged bow doors. *Lam Giang's* pumps labored to keep ahead of the rising flood. Nevertheless, after midnight, the vessel passed the port of Vung Tau, now at least partially in enemy hands, and then headed out into open ocean. Even with safety just ahead, the refugees held their breath expecting shells to perforate the steel hull at any moment. But all was quiet. The South China Sea was placid like a millpond.

As with the other refugees, Pham and his family had fled with virtually nothing—no food, no clothing except what they wore, and only a bottle of water for their young boy. Few on board had much more than the bare essentials. Some shared small containers of rice. A rumor spread among the refugees that they were headed to Con Son Island, a former penal colony, to rendezvous with the remnants of the Vietnamese navy.

Throughout the day and with a fierce tropical sun beating down upon them, this mass of humanity suffered from dehydration and hunger. The vessel's wretchedly clogged, filthy toilets had long ceased to function under the impossible demand. All on board suffered the indignity of relieving themselves in any buckets they could find. Down by the bow and with the steering problem still unresolved, the tired old LSM plodded southward. The ramshackle ship twisted back and forth like a snake through the water with its bilge pumps struggling to keep the vessel afloat.

As the green wooded hills of Con Son Island appeared off the starboard bow, exhausted and terrified refugees wondered what awaited them. In the sheltered bay, they could make out the motley fleet of gray South Vietnamese warships, colorful fishing boats, and smaller craft that had sought a haven in the anchorage.

"When that ship came over the horizon heading toward us, it was on our port side," recalled Chief Engineer Doyle. "The lookout said, 'Here comes a small boat.' Well, it wasn't a small boat. It was probably about 200 feet long. It appeared to be weaving its way and was very down by the bow. There was also a flashing light coming from it signaling that it needed help and that it was sinking. They were steering that sinuous course because they were forced to steer by hand. The motors that drove the big steering units would not work so they had jury-rigged the rudder to try to get it amidships but they couldn't. The rudder kept flopping back and forth. Another problem was that it was a twin-screw ship, and only one engine was functioning and driving only one of the screws."[7]

Doyle then added, "We went over to them and put our motor whaleboat in the water. Several of our people then boarded, including HMC Burwinkel. It was very clear that they knew they were sinking. They just couldn't pump the water out."[8]

Dam Thuy Nguyen's escape was no less dramatic. The young schoolteacher from Saigon was named for the river that flowed near where she was born in central Vietnam. "Dam Thuy also means pure water," she pointed out.[9] Nguyen grew up in Hue and attended a Catholic private school. And she had hopes: "My dream was to be a doctor, but I was really afraid of blood so instead I became a French teacher at the very prestigious Institute Lasan Taberd in Saigon."[10]

Following graduation she taught in public schools and continued doing so until 1974 when the minister of education in Saigon selected her to teach Vietnamese children at Peace Village in West Germany. Her departure date was February 1975, but since the school year ended in the middle of April, she requested a delay. That postponement would change her life.

In March 1975 South Vietnam's struggle for survival was under way. By early that month the situation had become critical. Each day the radio broadcast another defeat, first in the Central Highlands—Banmethuot, Pleiku, and then Kontum. Later that month, cities fell like dominoes from north to south—Danang, Quangtri, Hue, and Nha Trang. It was just a matter of time before the invaders swallowed up all of South Vietnam. But a well-to-do family with connections had a way out: bribing the right government official with gold. So arrangements were made for the Nguyen family to leave Saigon.

"We received the manifest with our name on it for the airplane with a flight number. A bus would pick us up behind the American embassy's back door at 1 o'clock on May 1 and take us to the airport. We would then show the manifest and they would take us on the plane."[11] But with the NVA on the outskirts of Saigon by April 27 and a twenty-four-hour curfew declared, the departure could not take place as planned. With the approaching sounds of battle, Nguyen, her widowed mother, three of her unmarried siblings, and several relatives remained in their home, afraid to venture outside. Virtual prisoners, the Nguyens kept track of developments.

"Then on the early morning of April 30, the radio officially announced that General Duong Van Minh, 'Big Minh,' had surrendered South Vietnam. Everybody looked at each other and that's the end of it. But our family still hoped with the manifest to wait for the next day and, hopefully, could still leave the country."[12] The family developed a complicated plan that would have them leaving the house one at a time and rendezvousing at noon near the American embassy. They would then board the bus near the site, as previously arranged, and go to the airport.

But because the city had already fallen to the North Vietnamese, the plan was more fantasy than practical strategy. VC troops were already in the neighborhood. As Nguyen opened the front door to step outside, she encountered two VC. One soldier looked vaguely familiar.

"I walked straight up to the communist soldier and tried to make friends. I said, 'Hello! Welcome. How are you?' I pretended to know him well and that I was happy to see him."[13] As it turned out, Nguyen did know one of these VC whose nephew had been her student. She continued talking with him to gain his confidence. He held a communist flag and was looking for a place to hang it.

"And right away that was a good reason for me to be flattering him. I said, 'Look, let me find a good place to help you hang this flag up. How about letting me do it?' He gave me the flag and I tried to find a place on the corner of my house." She continued in this obsequious tone by asking the VC, "Don't you think it would look nice up there?"[14]

But Nguyen didn't voice her innermost thoughts and instead tried to outsmart the soldier by playing up to his naiveté: "I just pretended nothing was happening but inside I'm boiling." The young soldier innocently responded to her smooth talk. "He then said, 'Yes. That's nice.'"[15]

She saw her opportunity. Feigning illness, she convinced the young fighter that she needed to go to the hospital, promising to return. Turning to his companion, the VC said, "Okay, we can let her go. She lives here. I know her."[16] Without further delay, she grabbed her young nephew, and the family chauffeur drove them in the direction of the hospital. Once clear of the two VC, she instructed the chauffeur to proceed to the rendezvous site where she waited in vain until noon for the arrival of the other family members.

Nguyen then recounted, "By then I started seeing North Vietnamese tanks driving around in front of our school, the Saigon cathedral, and the post office, and not far from the president's palace. I saw them run over people and kill them. I then realized it was too late to wait and I don't have time to waste. I had to be brave and told my nephew, 'Come on, let's go!'"[17] Nguyen, her nephew, and the chauffeur drove aimlessly through Saigon's chaotic streets not knowing where to go next. They spotted a man in a car waving at her and motioning for them to follow.

"I didn't know who he was but we followed him and then several cars followed me. We drove around like a parade along the river shore until we arrived at the Vietnamese navy camp along the Saigon River. The car ahead of me then stopped and people got out and ran down to the river's edge and jumped onto one boat. My nephew and I ran after them. The boat was high and very hard to get up. But we finally climbed up and I saw the number 402. I called it my 'Destiny Boat.'"[18]

As with Pham, Nguyen was one of thousands of refugees on board *Lam Giang*, and her experiences in many ways mirrored his death-defying encounters. Then she witnessed a darker side of human nature: people trying to take advantage of the desperate food shortages. "Someone from the Vietnamese navy stole some rice and kept it hidden on the boat. Later in the voyage he brought it out and sold it. That's how we finally got some rice."[19]

That the landing craft was taking on water through its partially closed bow doors was not lost on any of the passengers. Nguyen remembered the fear of that scene: "People were trying to get helmets, pots and pans, and whatever, to bail out the water from the boat. But what was coming in was more than what was going out. It was hard to make a chain to throw the water out because it was so crowded."[20]

To Nguyen, Pham, and many other refugees, it was never clear who was in charge or where they were headed. One refugee produced a portable radio and had it tuned to a Saigon station, drawing a large crowd around him. The announcer mentioned *Lam Giang* by name as having been stolen and demanded that the ship return to Saigon. Another man, who identified himself as a surgeon, had brought a book containing naval signaling instructions. He spent a great deal of time trying to determine how to signal another vessel for help. Nguyen noted how intent the man was, going so far as to use a woman's makeup mirror and a flashlight to give lighted warning signs in the darkness. He did this signaling for hours until the flashlight battery eventually gave out.

Con Son Island finally appeared at daybreak the following morning. *Lam Giang* approached the fleet—and none too soon. The landing craft wallowed in the gentle swells with her one operating engine idling to slow the incoming sea. Her bilge pumps were losing the battle, and it was apparent to all on board that the vessel was sinking.

The ship's dangerous condition was certainly evident to the sailors of USS *Kirk*, which came upon the dilapidated LSM and stood by to render assistance. *Kirk* radioed the Vietnamese flagship *Tran Nhat Duat* (HQ-3), which was about three miles ahead of *Kirk* at the time, and the vessel turned around to help. No sooner were lines made fast between the Vietnamese vessels than *Kirk* dispatched its motor whaleboat. Several crew members boarded the LSM, including HMC Stephen Burwinkel and his assistant HM3 Mark Falkenberg. Both corpsmen were eager to provide medical assistance, and they got to work without delay to assess the situation. Burwinkel had noted immediately that the ship was very down by the bow.

"You do realize that your ship is sinking," he pointed out to the South Vietnamese lieutenant on the bridge he judged to be in command.[21] The young officer nodded. He was well aware of his vessel's plight. In fact, HQ-3's intention was to transfer the refugees as quickly as possible.

Personnel from *Tran Nhat Duat*, which was the former U.S. Coast Guard high-endurance cutter *Yakutat*, rigged several rickety makeshift wooden planks between the two ships. They then instructed the refugees to proceed one at a time across the narrow bridge. Inching their way along that thin lifeline of planks was a lot to ask of exhausted and terrified refugees who ranged in age from the very young to the elderly. Yet all seemed to proceed without incident until a commotion involving much pushing and shoving suddenly developed among the refugees nearest the planks. A man had panicked, rushed forward, and knocked a young girl from the improvised "bridge" into the water. Before anyone could react, she was crushed between the two vessels. Instantly a Vietnamese naval officer drew his pistol, shot the offender in the back of the head, and kicked his body into the sea.

"It was a tragic thing to witness," remembered Burwinkel, "but his action cost him his life."[22] Wartime justice on the high seas had restored order and prevented a far greater disaster. The plank bridge was scarcely adequate to transfer several thousand refugees from one vessel to another. Some of the younger, more athletic refugees dared to jump on board the larger ship.

The slight Thuy Nguyen at first thought better of making the attempt and recalled, "I was almost thirty then and never did sports or knew how to jump very high."[23] Someone on board HQ-3 yelled to her, "Throw that boy over and I will catch him." She refused, noting how frequently the two vessels banged together and then moved apart. "If we miss, he would drop into the ocean and that would be the end of it," she quickly realized.[24] But the man was insistent, shouting, "Throw him over!" In desperation, Nguyen found a piece of rope and, leaving many feet of slack, tied her nephew to one end and herself to the other.

"'If anything happens, we both go,' I thought. When the boat came very close, my nephew, who was a very brave boy, jumped. The two men who were standing on the other boat caught him. Then it was my turn and I jumped over. I sat there shaking like I was in outer space and began to cry. 'We can never see our family again. But now my nephew is counting on me. I am everything to him. He will be the last person to carry on my family name so I have to protect him. I have no choice. I have to be brave to myself and my family. No more crying.'"[25]

After all the refugees were safely on board HQ-3 and it had pulled away, the beaten-up derelict *Lam Giang* slipped beneath the South China Sea.

Lan Nguyen Tran was seventeen in April 1975, a resident of Saigon, married to a Vietnamese air force pilot twelve years her senior, and about to give birth to her first child. Her grandparents, refugees from North Vietnam, had moved south with the great migration following partition in 1954. She recalled her family's fears about communism, saying, "My grandparents knew about communists and knew we could not live with them."[26] Nor could Lan live under terror. As Saigon descended into chaos with the imminent arrival of the NVA, she and her extended family had already planned their getaway.

Preparations had begun weeks before. Together they purchased a small boat, which they had moored on the Saigon River. If and when the capital fell, they would rendezvous at the dock and head downriver. But they didn't discuss what might happen once they reached the open sea. As the NVA surrounded the city on April 28, Lan's husband, on duty with his unit at Tan Son Nhut Air Base, called and told her grandparents that the time had come. They were all to meet at the boat and depart as quickly as possible. But Lan, her mother, and an uncle were already at the airport trying to get a flight out when incoming rockets and mortars pocked the runways, making the airport unusable. Just after midnight, the trio abandoned Tan Son Nhut Airport. Lan's husband chose to remain with his unit, at least for the present time. "It's no good for a soldier to leave," he told his young wife.[27]

Since Lan was due any time, her mother suggested they go to the hospital. But Saigon was in chaos. Thousands of refugees who had fled the fighting up north clogged the streets. Fires burned out of control. Looters lugging TVs, radios, and even mattresses vied with demoralized South Vietnamese soldiers who had stripped off their uniforms and joined in the pillage. Not a few had rape on their minds. It was questionable if any government still existed in the capital.

Lan and her mother sought the uncertain comfort of what had until recently been her grandparents' home, which was now empty. Both women felt overcome with loneliness and fear. In reality the house no longer belonged to the family. Her grandmother had sold it just days before and had taken payment in U.S. dollars, "insurance" the matriarch hoped would aid in their escape.

Very early the next morning after a mostly sleepless night, the two women welcomed a driver who showed up at the front door. He knew the family and had at least some reassuring news. The family boat was still at the dock—nothing to worry about. Would he take them there, Lan asked. He agreed but they would have to wait until that evening.

The driver returned as promised around 9 p.m., and they piled into his car with only a few possessions they could carry. "It was raining and storming and people were running. It was very hard to get through the traffic," Lan recalled.[28] Finally they reached the river, but then the young woman's heart sank. The family boat had left without them. Suppressing growing panic, she scanned the far riverbank and saw what appeared to be the missing craft. She asked the driver if he thought that was their boat, and he nodded.

Plunging into the river and swimming to the far side briefly crossed her mind, but the distance was too great. Lan knew she would never make it in her condition. And what about her mother? A small group of men approached wearing uniforms and waving their weapons. One asked the driver if he would like to rent a small boat to get across the river. "You don't have to pay much. Anything will be okay," one of the soldiers assured him.[29]

Lan clutched a small bag containing some money and what remained of her mother's jewelry. But before they agreed to any deal, one of the men snatched the bag from her and ran, the driver in hot pursuit. She shouted for him to stop, fearing they would shoot him. The driver reluctantly gave up the chase. And then they quickly realized that no such small boat existed to get them across the Saigon River.

"But suddenly—it happened like that—I saw the boat from the other side of the river come over to where we were," Lan called to mind as if it were just yesterday. "I was very glad. I said, 'Hey, the boat is here!'"[30] The boat cautiously approached the river's edge, but boulders, which had been deposited on the riverbank to resist erosion, made the situation very hazardous. "I could not get in the boat because of the rocks on the riverbank, which were very slippery. My mom say our names and then three of my husband's cousins helped me climb on the boat."[31]

The miracle of the craft's appearance, as it turned out, had been accidental. Earlier that afternoon, a man desperate to escape—who had little or no experience in operating Lan's family boat—managed to get the boat under way. But high water had prevented the small craft from proceeding beneath one of Saigon's many bridges. So this party of escapees had to return to their starting point to wait for the river to drop. Lan's timing had been fortuitous because it was at this point that she saw the boat make a second attempt to go downriver. Shortly after Lan, her mother, and their driver had boarded, they passed under the bridge with just feet to spare.

But the group was not yet out of danger. Tracer rounds lit the night sky and the staccato of automatic weapons punctuated the war-ravaged atmosphere. Small arms fire and rocket-propelled grenades had already hit some escaping refugees, making it difficult to determine whether communist troops or disgruntled South Vietnamese soldiers had been the source. Many deserters were firing their weapons in frustration and rage.

"The gunfire was very loud to scare us, but finally the boat was able to get down to the ocean," Lan remembered with a hint of panic still in her voice.[32]

Reaching the South China Sea offered relief from the violence but no respite from anxiety and uncertainty. What now? Although the seas were calm, the refugees faced a very uncertain future. Lan suddenly began to feel the first twinges of labor, but the pains were transitory and soon subsided. "Luckily, I don't have the baby, just the labor pains."[33] Later that day, April 30, the refugees watched a large American warship approach. It was USS *Kirk*. At the time, Lan was curled up, trying to get some rest, and felt the boat begin to rock.

"Then I look up from the bottom of the boat to see this very big ship. I don't even see the whole picture of the ship, just some of it. In my heart I know that this must be American ship. They brought us food, water, and everyone was so grateful and happy because we know that we will survive and the Americans would help us. Then they told us they would return."[34]

Before *Kirk* returned, the Vietnamese navy ship *Ly Thuong Kiet* (HQ-16) came alongside and transferred Lan and the other refugees to the larger vessel. The former U.S. Coast Guard cutter *Chincoteague* was mostly empty and had ample room for its new passengers. Crewmen of the 310-foot ship shared their meager rations with the refugees until USS *Kirk*'s motor whaleboat returned, as promised, with food, water, medical assistance—and hope.

EIGHT

CON SON RENDEZVOUS

"**S**OMEONE TAPPED ME on the shoulder and said, 'Pull the chart for Con Son Island,'" recalled former OS James Bongaard. He turned around to question the officer behind him, Lt. Jerry Kolman. "Where the heck is Con Son Island?" Bongaard dug down through his charts and pulled one out of the island.

Lieutenant Kolman, *Kirk's* operations officer, responded, "We're plotting a course for Con Son Island. We're going down there to do something according to what Captain Jacobs wants." "Who else is going with us?" Bongaard asked. "Who are we following?" He knew *Kirk* usually followed a carrier and the ship rarely cruised by itself. And more to the point, the entire Seventh Fleet Task Force 76 was right there. But he wasn't prepared for the officer's answer: "We're going down alone."[1]

At approximately 10:30 p.m. on April 30, *Kirk* left the Vung Tau holding area and set a course for Con Son Island, approximately 115 miles southwest of the South Vietnamese port of Vung Tau. As she took her new heading and pulled away from the fleet at a leisurely ten knots, the destroyer escort showed no signs of being in any kind of hurry. *Kirk's* goal was to steam in darkness and arrive at sunrise. "We sailed what was left of the night," Richard Armitage stated, "and as dawn broke, we were at Con Son Island."[2]

To *Kirk's* crew, the Manhattan-size island—thirteen miles long and five miles wide—resembled an island paradise crowned with low mountains covered by green vegetation. But its appearance was deceiving. During the French colonial period, Con Son had been turned into a penal colony, earning the reputation as the "Devil's Island of Southeast Asia." After 1954, following the first Indochina war, the South Vietnamese used the island for the same purpose, housing political prisoners and criminal offenders. Ironically the once dreaded island now offered temporary sanctuary to about fifty Vietnamese navy ships and thousands of refugees fleeing their homeland.

Lt. Bob Lemke, a material officer on the Destroyer Squadron 23 staff, recalled his first impression: "They were all there floating out across the horizon. Then I knew that we had gotten to the rendezvous. It was quite impressive to see a parking lot full of ships."[3] Lemke saw a motley assortment of vessels, most of which had been American leftovers from World War II and Korea—Navy and Coast Guard craft ranging from landing ships to vessels called WHECs (high-endurance cutters). Sprinkled among this hodgepodge of former U.S. ships were fishing boats and more modern patrol craft, including swift boats that had seen action in the Mekong Delta.

Awed by the scene, Capt. Paul Jacobs recounted, "As we approached, we could see their fleet. Some were anchored. Others were dead in the water or adrift. And the ships were just loaded with refugees, some with people all the way up to the bridge. Many had been out there for a week or so with no water and no food. It seemed that this was going to be an insurmountable problem. I said to myself, 'Oh my God, how are we going to pull this off?'"[4]

Armitage, architect of the evacuation plan, was more relieved than concerned. "We saw just what was a wonderful sight to my eyes—scores of Vietnamese ships and an awful lot of people on board them. And they were waiting there as Captain Kiem and I had discussed twenty-four hours before."[5]

Phase one—the rendezvous with the South Vietnamese fleet—had been accomplished. *Kirk* was now in a position to carry out Armitage's master plan. He related, "The *Kirk* could communicate with the rest of the U.S. fleet and go with us across to the Philippines and be able to rescue any folks who might be in harm's way. Some had been wounded. Some were pregnant. All were sick and I needed some way to take care of those folks. For me, the *Kirk* was perfect."[6]

The first order of business was to establish communications with the South Vietnamese ships and for *Kirk*'s motor whaleboat to ferry Armitage over to *Tran Nhat Duat* (HQ-3), the designated flagship for what remained of the Vietnamese navy. From that former U.S. Coast Guard cutter, he and the last chief of naval operations of the Vietnamese navy, Vice Admiral Chung Tan Cang, would monitor the exodus east across the South China Sea to the Philippines.

"When we looked closely," recollected Chief Engineer Hugh Doyle, "we saw that all these ships were just packed to the gills with refugees—peasants, Navy people, fishermen, everything." They had come from all up and down the coast.[7] Some vessels, which had been out of food and had been rationing water, requested provisions from *Kirk*. The warship's motor whaleboat sent the much-needed food, water, and medical supplies. Despite the terribly crowded conditions, Vietnamese navy personnel had managed to maintain discipline on board the ships.

Doyle noted that this improved state of affairs was in sharp contrast to what had occurred in the preceding weeks when South Vietnam had quickly succumbed to enemy forces. Tens of thousands of panicked refugees fleeing the coastal cities had crowded on board transports and even barges towed by tugboats. One ship, intended to carry a crew of 18, had taken on board an estimated 12,000 refugees. Chaotic radio intercepts from those evacuation ships told of Vietnamese army deserters selling scarce water supplies to refugees. Firefights between rival soldiers broke out on some of these vessels over food and water, and refugees were often caught in the crossfire. Many were killed and thrown unceremoniously into the sea.

Conditions were almost indescribable, according to Lt. Cdr. Daniel Daly, an aide to Rear Adm. Donald Whitmire: "[There] were armed government deserters or Vietnamese soldiers somehow separated from their units among the refugees. We were afraid that fights would break out on those ships. We had visions of soldiers machine-gunning someone, with a thousand people standing behind the targets being hit by the bullets that missed. There was no place for anyone to go."[8]

Daly noted that fatalities on those ships began rising to alarming levels. After Vietnamese army deserters hijacked MS *Greenville Victory* on April 3, Rear Admiral Whitmire put squads of U.S. Marines on board the merchant ships to protect the crews. Daly recorded a radio exchange between Whitmire and one of those Marines on board the contract ship MS *Transcolorado*:

ADMIRAL: Son, this is Admiral Whitmire. I want you to tell me what conditions are really like in your ship.

MARINE: Begging your pardon, sir, but I am currently standing in two inches of shit. There are no latrines on this ship for the refugees. They just squat where they are. The stench is unbelievable.

There's a freshwater hose running up the deck to the bow where there is a bunch of Vietnamese soldiers with a lot of guns. They are selling drinks of water. They watch my guys and we watch them. But I think that hundreds will get killed if we start a firefight, so we haven't interfered with their operation.

About two hours ago I saw a baby being born. As its head came out of the mother, it plowed a furrow in the shit on the deck. About ten minutes ago, I saw the bodies of both the baby and the mother thrown overboard. Someone gets thrown overboard about every fifteen minutes.

Daly vividly remembered, "I watched tears flow down Admiral Whitmire's face as he listened. We all knew we were witnessing a world-class tragedy."[9]

Whitmire's approval of Armitage's evacuation plan may well have been influenced by this harrowing experience. If the initial plan was to rescue the Vietnamese navy, Armitage had said nothing on board *Kirk* the previous night about a humanitarian component—and certainly not of the magnitude this small warship and its crew now faced. Despite his shock, Captain Jacobs immediately began turning his man-of-war into an assistance ship. He announced over the 1MC: "[Our mission is] going to be purely humanitarian." But then he posed the seemingly unanswerable question to his officers: "How are we going to help these 30,000 people get out of a war-torn country into a safe place?"[10]

Following his briefing with the crew, Jacobs began implementing his own plan. He immediately dispatched members of his Engineering Department and his chief engineer, Lt. Hugh Doyle, to the South Vietnamese naval vessels for an assessment of the situation. A few of the ships had been in the navy yard in Saigon for overhaul when the end came. These ships had escaped with engines needing service and carrying few spare parts. Nevertheless, *Kirk*'s engineers soon discovered that the South Vietnamese crews, for the most part, were quite capable of operating their vessels. After all, most of the vessels had made it this far to Con Son Island.

Throughout that Thursday, May 1, and the following day, *Kirk*'s motor whaleboat shuttled back and forth with supplies. But the most important task was to get the ships under way as soon as possible, well out into international waters and presumably further out of danger. The orders were to take a compass heading of 090 degrees—due east—and rendezvous at a second holding area about one hundred miles east of Con Son Island.

One after another, engines sputtered to life, spewing greasy blue diesel smoke from their exhausts. But getting some of these tired old ships moving was not an easy task. "Sometimes we couldn't even pull the anchors up," Jacobs related.[11] In those stubborn cases, the crews ran the ships forward over their anchors in an effort to break them loose from the bottom. In a few instances, an acetylene cutting torch severed the rusty anchor chain and the vessel got under way minus its anchor.

Thirty Vietnamese navy ships and boats plus two civilian fishing trawlers comprised the "official" number of ships in the Con Son anchorage. But an estimated fifty other vessels, including small river patrol boats, were present, not counting many small fishing boats. Many of the smaller craft were clearly unsuitable for an ocean voyage.

That first day at Con Son, Vietnamese navy personnel determined which ships were capable of making the transit and which vessels would be left behind once their passengers were transferred to larger seaworthy ships. *Kirk* had very little to do with this operation. The scene just off Con Son Island soon resembled the roundup stage of a cattle drive with *Kirk* herding the thirty-two South Vietnamese naval vessels and other craft into a very loose formation.

Shortly after 2 p.m. on May 2, *Kirk*'s log indicated that the warship had been "detached to proceed to Subic Bay."[12] "It was a confusing, busy period of fits and starts with the entire USN/VNN formation gradually moving to the east and southeast, slowly away from Con Son Island throughout the remainder of the day," Doyle called to mind.[13] Those "fits and starts" escalated for Jacobs and his crew. Rather than leading the formation on a steady easterly course, *Kirk* flitted about like a border collie, channeling errant vessels together and reacting to one crisis after another.

One of these diversions involved a white-hulled luxury cabin cruiser, which was about 50 feet in length, with *Triton II* emblazoned across her transom. Some *Kirk* crew members boarded the motor whaleboat to investigate. They found five Vietnamese on board an apparently spanking new yacht with gleaming mahogany brightwork. The men claimed to be boatyard workers from Saigon where the cabin cruiser had been built for a wealthy European. But Doyle doubted the workers' assertion that they had tried to "save" the boat for the new owner.

He observed, "They clearly could have cared less about it once they were on board *Kirk*. I'm sure they simply stole it."[14] Nevertheless, Jacobs allowed them to tie up alongside and come on board as refugees.

Triton II impressed Doyle and the other crew members, with Doyle excitedly recounting, "It was absolutely beautiful! It had a ferro-cement hull, and the interior was all solid mahogany and teak. It was an awesome bit of craftsmanship that looked like it was finished out by a world-class cabinetmaker. There was a bar inside, three sit-down tables . . . [and] two great big diesel engines."[15] Rather than casting the pleasure craft adrift, Captain Jacobs made a quick decision to salvage and use it to augment *Kirk*'s overworked motor whaleboat and gig. After inspecting it for booby traps, *Triton II* was refueled and a small "prize crew" put on board. The newly acquired addition to the flotilla took station one hundred yards off *Kirk*'s starboard quarter.

"The captain was getting a bit impatient with the *Triton II* delay," Doyle recalled, "and he was anxious to come up in speed so we could overtake the formation. As we increased speed, *Triton II* also came up in speed to keep station with us. Suddenly there came a shout from the prize crew that the boat was on fire! *Kirk* stopped. As we were preparing to send a 'rescue and assistance' team to fight the fire on the boat, the crew reported that the fire was out. Someone on board had finally located a CO_2 fire extinguisher and smothered the flames. Because it was an engine compartment fire, the boat was now out of commission, and we started to make preparations to tow it."[16]

But *Kirk*'s skipper, already stressed by the increasing tempo of activity, was not amused by this latest delay. And now a Vietnamese fishing boat approached with some Vietnamese navy enlisted sailors and their families, indicating that they, too, wanted to be taken on board. All passengers came onto the ship except for the captain who decided to return with his boat to South Vietnam. *Kirk* was dead in the water and falling farther behind the vessels she was supposed to be leading.

Jacobs' slow boil suddenly turned to anger. He had had enough of *Triton II* and ordered the prize crew to return to *Kirk*. Doyle never forgot the indelible image of the incongruous white yacht with her varnished mahogany embellishments: "[We watched it] drifting forlornly astern of *Kirk* as we rapidly pulled away."[17]

After *Kirk* cast the hard-luck yacht adrift, she was finally able to make up for lost time and close the distance to the fleet of South Vietnamese ships some ten miles ahead. A helicopter, which was from one of the formation's World War II–era LSTs, suddenly took off and landed on *Kirk* a short time later. On board the helo were a Vietnamese air force pilot and copilot, a naval officer from the LST, and a Vietnamese navy SEAL commander, who seemed to be in charge.[18] They desperately needed food and medical supplies to take back to the ship, which they said had at least three thousand refugees packed on board.

When their helicopter had flown out to the LST from Can Tho the previous day as the city was being overrun, they had taken enemy fire, and a few bullets had ripped through the helo. Miraculously, neither the passengers nor the engine had been hit. Not only would the helicopter crew receive the requested food and medical supplies, but *Kirk*'s men would also refuel their bird and make it ready for a quick return to the LST. "We encouraged the helo crew to go below and get something to eat and drink and relax for a few minutes," related Lt. Rick Sautter, "while the helo was being refueled."[19] Despite what appeared to be only superficial damage—a few bullet holes through the helo's skin—no one noticed how badly the fuel tank had been shot up.

As ADJC Glen Bingham plugged in the fueling hose and started to put pressure in the tank, Sautter noted that "fuel began streaming out everywhere. It was like one of those cartoons where someone has been machine-gunned, then takes a drink of water, and the water shoots out from all the holes in his body. We turned off the fuel and threw the helicopter over the side."[20]

The Vietnamese pilot and copilot and the SEAL commander came topside from the wardroom after having refreshed themselves only to discover that their aircraft was gone. Doyle recalled that they were very disturbed "until we told them what was wrong—that when they arrived aboard, they had five minutes of gas left."[21] The pilot calmed down, perhaps thankful he had landed when he did.

USS *Kirk* (DE-1087) enters the
Mississippi River on her launch
day, September 25, 1971.

Kirk receives supplies from a
CH-46 helicopter while under
way.

Kirk's CO, Lt. Cdr. Paul Jacobs

AN Gerald McClellan coaxes the first South Vietnamese Huey onto *Kirk*'s flight deck.
HUGH DOYLE

Commander Jacobs (*third from left*) helps push a Huey over the side.

Balanced on the warship's deck edge

Another Huey falls into
the South China Sea.
KENT CHIPMAN

Packed with terri-
fied refugees, a Huey
passes across the
destroyer escort's
fantail.
HUGH DOYLE

Sailor comforts a refugee.
HUGH DOYLE

Crewmen frantically wave off the CH-47 Chinook as it attempts to land.
Craig Compiano

Passengers jump to the deck from the copilot's door.

Chinook hovers with its tires in the water as pilot Major Ba Nguyen prepares to ditch.
HUGH DOYLE

The huge helicopter explodes as its rotors impact the water.
HUGH DOYLE

The capsized aircraft reminded crewman MMFN Kent Chipman of a dead armadillo. Pilot Ba Nguyen appears at lower right.

Hugh Doyle

Kirk's motor whaleboat approaches the ship with the rescued pilot on board.

Hugh Doyle

Richard Armitage and Vietnamese friends
RICHARD ARMITAGE

Captain Kiem Do worked
with Richard Armitage to
set the evacuation plan in
motion.
KIEM DO

A very crowded flight deck greets Armitage as he lands on USS *Blue Ridge* (LCC-19).

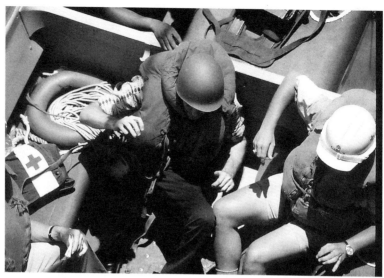

HM3 Mark Falkenberg (*left*) and HMC Stephen Burwinkel head for *Lam Giang* (HQ-402) on board *Kirk's* motor whaleboat to lend a hand.
JAMES BONGAARD

Transfer of refugees from the overcrowded and sinking *Lam Giang* to the Vietnamese flagship *Tran Nhat Duat* (HQ-3).
JAMES BONGAARD

HMC Stephen Burwinkel was responsible for the health of nearly 32,000 refugees.
STEPHEN BURWINKEL

VNN minesweeper *Chi Linh* (HQ-11), with her decks crammed with refugees, steams just off *Kirk*'s starboard side.
HUGH DOYLE

U.S. Air Force to the rescue: an HC-130 approaches *Kirk*.
Hugh Doyle

The HC-130 drops the first of two 55-gallon drums filled with much-needed medical supplies.
Hugh Doyle

A young refugee manages a smile despite her circumstances.
JAMES BONGAARD

South Vietnamese naval personnel throw ordnance overboard in compliance with the
re-flagging agreement.
HUGH DOYLE

Crewmen of the patrol vessel *Van Kiep II* (HQ-14) sing the South Vietnamese national anthem for the last time as their flag is lowered.
LIEM BUI

The U.S. flag is raised, officially transferring the ship to U.S. Navy command.
Liem Bui

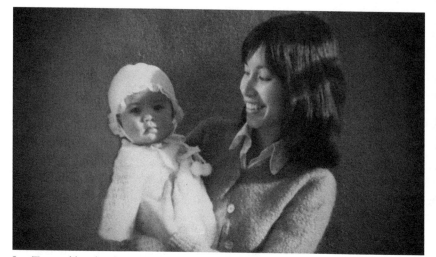

Lan Tran and her daughter, Tien, shortly after they arrived in the United States
LAN TRAN

Lan Tran and her daughter at Tien's college graduation in 2000
LAN TRAN

NINE

HOUSE CALLS

As *KIRK*'s CREW herded the South Vietnamese fleet together and worked expeditiously to get the overloaded ships under way to the Philippines, the situation was anything but certain. How would the North Vietnamese victors react to the potential escape of what remained of the Vietnamese navy and its personnel? The destroyer escort was well equipped to fight Soviet submarines, but with its single 5-inch deck gun, the ship would be difficult to defend against fast-flying hostile aircraft. "This country now belonged to someone else," pointed out Capt. Paul Jacobs. "They had access to the aircraft we had given to the South Vietnamese. We were like sitting ducks. They could have taken off and taken out the *Kirk* and all the Vietnamese ships if they wanted to. We had no idea how they were going to react."[1]

As if to punctuate that apprehension, an unidentified low-flying jet appeared off *Kirk*'s starboard bow. Fearing an attack by what appeared to be a captured A-37 attack aircraft, general quarters was sounded. A strident voice resonated throughout the ship: "This is not a drill! Air threat! Low flyer reported off starboard bow!" Men scurried to their battle stations and prepared for the worst. Fortunately the friendly aircraft, which probably had a malfunctioning transponder and could not identify itself, flew on. The crewmen then refocused their attention on the task at hand—aiding refugees.

By Friday morning, May 2, *Kirk* and her sister ship, USS *Cook* (DE-1083), had arrived at the newest rendezvous about one hundred miles east of Con Son Island to lend a hand. Both ships soon had the convoy under way and heading east. The five-mile-long formation of Vietnamese navy vessels consisted of two sixteen-ship columns, each file about a mile apart.

The two escorts could steam only as fast as the slowest vessel in the convoy, a speed that would seldom exceed five knots. With its unreliable power plant, the overcrowded coastal freighter *Tan Nam Viet*, which was not a part of the formal thirty-two-ship Vietnamese navy formation, shadowed *Kirk*. The freighter was seeking protection of the American man-of-war and dependent on the destroyer escort's generosity for food, water, and fuel. A few unseaworthy fishing boats also followed in *Kirk*'s wake.

Keeping *Tan Nam Viet* moving under its own power proved very challenging. On that Friday morning, someone on board the ship signaled in broken English that the ship was flooding and its pumps could not keep up with the rising water.

Chief Engineer Hugh Doyle, BTC Wallace Michaelson, and several other enlisted engineers went on board to pump up her fuel service tanks, repair the vessel's auxiliary boiler, and restart the main engine that had been starved for fuel. When they tried to determine a cause for the flooding, they discovered the ship had been taking in some water through a stern tube. But no crew member on that merchant ship could figure out how to start the pump needed to force the accumulated water overboard.

"We showed them how to start their pump, and pump it out," Doyle remembered. "It turned out they weren't really flooding at all. And that was one catastrophe taken care of." Doyle said that the Vietnamese ship, which carried between six hundred and seven hundred refugees, had left Saigon "in such haste that none of their own engineers were onboard, save one little old 'wiper,' whose most complicated job previously had been running tea and mopping up spilled oil!"[2]

As the engineers crawled among a maze of piping in the engine room, they soon learned that the three-year-old vessel had been built in Japan and all the instruction plates were in both Japanese and Vietnamese. Whatever technical manuals they could find were also bilingual—Japanese and Vietnamese. "So there was a lot of hit-or-miss tracing of systems," Doyle recounted.[3] Given the confusion in the engine room, the chief engineer called for reinforcements after he realized that his small repair team needed assistance on *Tan Nam Viet*. Doyle related that his team was just "groping around in the dark to sort out that very strange ship."[4]

The new team arrived by gig led by *Kirk*'s XO, Lieutenant Commander McKenna. With him were a half dozen men, including the red-bearded main propulsion assistant, Lt.(jg) John Pine; BTC John Gornto, who was another highly experienced chief boiler technician; and HMC Stephen Burwinkel, *Kirk*'s chief hospital corpsman, who brought medical supplies. Doyle remembered that the newcomers faced a much more complicated task of replacing the main diesel engine's massive cylinder head.

As with the ill-fated yacht, the *Tan Nam Viet*, which was again lagging behind the main formation, proved to be another major distraction for *Kirk*. As *Kirk* poured on steam in pursuit, a tugboat tied alongside *Tan Nam Viet* ran its engines at full throttle trying to keep the merchant ship moving toward the convoy. Meanwhile the repair team labored below to get *Tan Nam Viet*'s main engine working again. At midnight, after finally arriving at the rendezvous area, *Kirk*'s repair team at last succeeded in fixing the freighter.

Doyle recalled the event:

At that time, the whole main deck was just covered with women and children and babies sleeping and mothers nursing their infants. They were all sleeping very soundly when we lit off the big engine. You could hear the roar and rumble and feel the vibrations all over the ship. I was standing on the main deck, and there must have been 150 babies crying their eyes out. The engine woke them and their mothers from a sound sleep, and it scared them half to death. I really felt bad but it was an amazing sight. Once we got the engine warmed up, we secured it again, the babies went back to sleep, and we let the ship drift the rest of the night. We all transferred back over to the *Kirk* a little before one in the morning, dirty, hot, tired, and thirsty.[5]

Early Saturday morning, May 3, *Kirk* radioed *Tan Nam Viet* and told whoever might be in charge to get under way on their own, "They were very reluctant to part company with us," Doyle called to mind, "but they did as they were told, and off they went over the horizon doing about ten knots—on their main engine under their own power."[6] All the ships were under way once again, heading toward the Philippines. With each mile gained, Doyle stated that "the entire idea of defending the convoy against attack just evaporated and it became taking the doc on house calls and delivering rice and delivering medicine."[7]

The "doc" he referred to was Burwinkel, a hospital corpsman with many years of experience under his belt and, no doubt, the best man for what seemed an impossible job. Before becoming part of *Kirk*'s commissioning crew in 1972, Burwinkel had already seen duty at a U.S. Navy hospital in Morocco, served on two ships, and tended wounded Marines in Vietnam. The thirty-four-year-old Cincinnati native was beloved by his crew not only for his cool, even temperament and wry sense of humor but also for the consummate skill he brought to his profession. Burwinkel was an independent duty corpsman, a highly trained health-care professional able to run the medical department on any Navy vessel without an assigned physician.

The "medical department" Burwinkel ruled on board *Kirk* was anything but spacious. Sick bay occupied a space about five by ten feet. "I had some cabinets, a small desk, and a table. There was enough room to have a patient and me or a patient and Petty Officer Falkenberg," Burwinkel mused. "It was a small setup."[8]

Doc Burwinkel's primary responsibility and that of his junior corpsman, HM3 Mark Falkenberg, was maintaining a healthy crew, a task that required constant vigilance. Any condition that might compromise health had their attention: sanitation, food preparation, water supply, training the crew in first aid, diagnosing and treating illness, and suturing wounds. The corpsmen even had to maintain the crew's immunization records and handle routine dental problems. Although an enlisted crew member and an independent duty corpsman, Burwinkel held a special status and reported directly to the CO. As the convoy and its two escorts prepared to get under way for Subic Bay on the afternoon of Friday, May 2, Burwinkel's skills and endurance would be tested beyond anyone's imagination.

Doyle noted the chief corpsman's stamina: "Chief Burwinkel was just tireless. He was a country doctor making house calls. But he had 30,000 patients and he didn't have a little jeep to drive around in. He had a boat."[9]

Burwinkel had indeed commandeered a swift boat—the small, shallow-draft patrol craft put to good use in the Mekong Delta during the war. He and several volunteers from *Kirk* cruised up and down the two columns of Vietnamese ships, stopping to hold sick call on board each one. Those volunteers included a boatswain's mate 1st class and sometimes one of *Kirk*'s other chiefs. They provided security on board the vessels and ensured that Burwinkel's prospective patients weren't armed.

"As we found weapons, over the side they went. I can't tell you the number of .38-caliber pistols, shotguns, and rifles that are on the bottom of the South China Sea," Burwinkel stated, never having forgotten the ever-present danger of armed Vietnamese.[10]

Another obstacle to overcome was the language barrier. Neither the chief corpsman nor any of his fellow sailors spoke Vietnamese. "A lot of it was hand signals. Usually I could find maybe one person who had at least some knowledge of English. As soon as they knew that I was what in Vietnamese was a *bacsi*—a 'doctor'—they would light up."[11] Burwinkel was always on the lookout for anyone on those vessels who might have medical training and could lend a hand.

"I discovered two Vietnamese officers on one of the ships we boarded who were physicians, one army and one navy. I thought, wow, this is a real fortune. And they were not only physicians but spoke excellent English. I told them what I was attempting to do and said that when I returned from the *Kirk*, I would bring back to them whatever supplies they needed, such as stethoscopes, blood pressure cuffs, etc. And they said, 'No. The war for us is finis, and we're finis with the war.'"[12]

Burwinkel related, still with a note of incredulousness in his voice, "I looked at them with some curiosity and said, 'You mean you won't lend your medical expertise to help these people?'" This three-way conversation abruptly ended with one of the Vietnamese doctors tersely saying, "No, the war is over. We're not doing anything. We're refugees like everybody else." The chief corpsman recounted in an irate tone, "I had a gun with me but fortunately I had no ammunition. And it's a good thing I didn't because I felt like shooting them both right on the spot. And that's the last I saw of them."[13]

Despite his short-lived anger and disbelief over this incident, Burwinkel continued on his rounds. "Sometimes I'd go back to the *Kirk* during the day to replenish my supplies such as ACE bandages, battle dressings, and other dressing materials and go back out. Usually about dark I'd come back aboard to get something to eat and change my clothes. Then I'd start out again the next morning. A few times because of certain circumstances, I spent significant time aboard some ships—sometimes all night. I didn't want to take the chance of finding the *Kirk* in the dark."[14]

On the second and third day, Burwinkel began encountering upper respiratory problems, which he treated as best he could. Miraculously he saw few trauma cases. One situation, however, was unusual: an older man with a bullet wound in his lower abdomen. "I could see his intestine and that's why I thought he couldn't survive but would probably die of peritonitis. I noticed that he had already been treated by someone. He had a dressing and what looked like sulfa powder sprinkled in the wound."[15]

A Vietnamese officer begged the corpsman to take the man back to *Kirk*, but Burwinkel was at a loss as to what could be done for him back on the ship with medical capabilities so limited. Nevertheless this older patient ended up on board *Kirk*. Burwinkel continued, "I really didn't know what to do with him but wait for him to die. I opened up the table in what we called the 'after battle dressing station' and inserted an IV. I then got a young [petty officer] 3rd class and showed him how to do blood pressures and change the IV. Then I said, 'This guy is yours until we reach the Philippines—or if he dies before then. Don't give him anything to drink except to wet his lips.'"[16]

But the old man refused to die. After *Kirk* arrived in the Philippines, he was admitted to the U.S. Naval Hospital in Subic Bay where he underwent surgery. "Afterward, he was doing fine—sitting up and smiling. He was a tough old man," Burwinkel added with a grin.[17]

An even more challenging patient came on board *Kirk* from the Vietnamese flagship *Tran Nhat Duat* (HQ-3) that Saturday morning just as the flotilla was getting under way. Chief Burwinkel immediately recognized the severity of his injury—a compound fracture of the femur. A jagged white end of fractured bone protruded through the skin threatening the leg's main blood vessels. Burwinkel knew right away that he was way out of his league. Without skilled orthopedic surgery, the man would surely lose the leg.

Burwinkel applied a splint to immobilize the fracture and then headed up to the bridge to confer with his CO. He told Jacobs that the patient needed to be evacuated to a vessel with surgical capabilities as soon as possible if he were to keep his leg.

Unfortunately, *Kirk* had no working helicopter on board to perform the medevac. Her LAMPS Seasprite helo was out of order in the hangar with a bad engine. Also, the Huey, which was tied down on the flight deck beside the hangar, had been involved in an accident that occurred on April 29. The main rotor of a Huey that was landing clipped the tail rotor gearbox of the parked Huey with nearly catastrophic results. An emergency radio call to USS *Cook* found that the LAMPS from that ship had already been dispatched for some other task. Moreover, even if that helicopter had been available, *Kirk*'s flight deck was then too crowded for it to land.

Jacobs called for Lt. Rick Sautter, the officer in charge of *Kirk*'s LAMPS detachment, to come to the bridge. Could his mechanics make that Huey, currently tethered to the deck, flyable? Sautter grinned. Indeed they could. The only reason they had kept it was because it was just too new and pristine to dump overboard. Days earlier, during all the frenetic helicopter activity, Sautter and his men had been on the lookout for a Huey with a good tail pylon they could remove. When a lull in the action occurred, his mechanics noted a serviceable Huey that had just landed and they removed the tail pylon, which included the drive shaft and tail rotor. Because the tail pylon on a Huey is held on by four bolts, the mechanics removed it in short order. They then dragged the tail pylon into the hangar next to the LAMPS helicopter for possible future use.

That foresight now paid off. PO1 Doug Ainsworth had previously worked on Hueys, and because Hueys were designed for battlefield repair, the work went quickly. After bolting on the spare pylon, he coupled the tail rotor drive shaft and synchronized the tail rotor drive. Crewmen then refueled and readied the "new" Huey with the dark green fuselage and faded green tail pylon for its mercy mission. With Sautter in the pilot seat and Lt. (jg) Scott Olin as his copilot, they took off for a ten-minute test flight near the ship. The Huey performed perfectly.

As Chief Burwinkel strapped himself and his patient's Stokes litter to the helo's deck, USS *Cook*'s LAMPS helicopter appeared overhead. It had completed its mission and was now available to accompany the restored Huey—just in case. Less than forty-five minutes after leaving *Kirk*, the helo returned, having delivered its patient to USS *Flint*.[18] The medevac to *Flint* was but a temporary diversion for Chief Burwinkel. Soon after returning, he was back in the motor whaleboat and off again on his rounds.

Among the huge refugee population, it was not unusual for Burwinkel to encounter pregnant women, some of whom were near term. When he mentioned this additional refugee complication to the CO, Jacobs suggested that these women be transferred to *Kirk*. Burwinkel noted, "I said, 'Skipper, we don't need any pregnant women on this ship.'" Not against caring for the expectant mothers, the experienced veteran asserted: "That possibility didn't really cause me any anxiety because part of my tour in Morocco included duty in the delivery room. The process of a woman giving birth wasn't fearful to me."[19]

But the chief corpsman realized that *Kirk* couldn't provide the necessary medical attention for several near-term mothers with accompanying post-delivery challenges. After a brief conference, however, Burwinkel and Jacobs agreed to transfer the women to *Kirk* where Burwinkel could deal with them early in the morning before he began his rounds among the ships in the Vietnamese fleet.

His assistant, who had heard about this decision, remarked to his boss, "Chief, what are we gonna do if one of these ladies has a baby?" Burwinkel retorted, "I assume we'll witness the miracle of birth, Petty Officer Falkenberg."[20]

The day after Joseph Pham and his family had been transferred from the sinking *Lam Giang* to the Vietnamese navy ship HQ-3, Burwinkel and his volunteers came on board bringing water, medical supplies, and food. The chief corpsman asked if anyone was sick and if any women might be pregnant. Pham, one of the few on board who spoke English, stepped forward and said that his wife was pregnant. Shortly thereafter Burwinkel's relief team transferred him, his wife, and young son to *Kirk*, along with four other expectant mothers.

"After so many days without food and water, we felt we had been released from the dead—like going from hell to heaven," Pham clearly remembered. "When we arrived aboard the *Kirk*, Captain Jacobs was one of the first people we met. He welcomed us and made sure the expecting mothers were treated and given proper care."[21] Pham quickly returned the favor by volunteering to serve on Chief Burwinkel's relief team as an interpreter, going from ship to ship. His skills were sorely needed and greatly appreciated.

No one appreciated Pham more than Lan Tran, who soon encountered him and the relief team when they boarded *Ly Thuong Kiet* (HQ-16). "Mr. Pham, the translator, said that the *Kirk* wanted to take people who were sick or those women who were over seven months pregnant to go aboard the USS *Kirk* for further medical attention. I didn't want to go because I didn't want to go alone. I wanted to stay with my mother. So they took both of us."[22]

For the anxious young woman, the transfer to *Kirk* was memorable. Several sailors strapped her into a Stokes wire litter and gently lowered her into the motor whaleboat. "It was a very dark night and was very scary. I thought, Oh my God! Maybe I will drop into the ocean! Then they took me to the *Kirk*. They put me in a basket and lifted me with some machine. It was very dark and all I could see were the orange vests the sailors were wearing. When I got there, I was so tired and again I had a labor pain."[23]

To accommodate the pregnant women, the *Kirk* crew converted a former lounge, which they called "The Ballroom," into a mini–maternity ward.

Lan continued, "They put me in a big room with four other pregnant women and their families. The next morning, Captain Jacobs came to our room for the first time. After that he come every day. He always smile. He told us he want at least one baby to be born on the ship and named after the USS *Kirk*."[24] In fact, whenever Jacobs visited these late-term women, he delivered a pep talk, encouraging them to get busy and start having their babies.

"They treat us very kindly and take good care of us," Lan reflected. "They make sure we have three meals a day and we ate the same food at the mess hall as . . . the other U.S. sailors. And they did our laundry, too."[25]

Jacobs ordered AW3 Don Cox to look after the women, accompany them to the galley for meals, and ensure that they got topside at least once a day for fresh air. While Burwinkel was on his rounds, the women were in the care of Hospital Corpsman 3rd Class Falkenberg who nervously monitored their condition, fearful that he would have to deliver a baby without his chief's assistance. That anxiety reached a fever pitch when one of the women went into labor; but her contractions stopped.[26]

With Falkenberg in charge of *Kirk*'s sick bay, Burwinkel went about his rounds from ship to ship. "Treating that many people was daunting enough to me," Burwinkel called to mind, "but I was young enough to have a big enough head that I wasn't afraid of that from a knowledge standpoint. The logistics, however, was an obstacle I wasn't sure I could overcome. The supplies I had on hand, the vast number of people that needed treatment, and the amount of time that it took . . . I didn't get a lot of sleep. I'd come back to the ship just before dark, grab a little bite to eat if I could, and get a little shuteye."[27]

Sometimes *Kirk*'s motor whaleboat served as Burwinkel's medical launch. Chief Engineer Doyle would recall him spending hours tending to the refugees. Doyle remembered Burwinkel with admiration, "How he did it is beyond me. To make a long story short, he's a wonderful man and a wonderful doctor, and he was absolutely what we needed at that time. He's not a doctor, of course. We call him 'Doc.' He's a very capable, independent duty hospital corpsman. I would have anointed him 'doctor' right after we got into Subic because of what he did."[28]

OS Jim Bongaard's affection for his corpsman was and still is indicative of the rest of the crew.

> Doc Burwinkel's responsibility for 30,000 or so Vietnamese was unheard of and we kept track of him as best we could, keeping in touch with the ships as he was going from one to the other back and forth. But he was such our beloved doc that we all were concerned about him. He'd have to wear a pistol on his hip because we still didn't know if they had any North Vietnamese on board these ships. And he'd be a prime target so we were very much concerned. He'd come back on board to get some supplies and then he'd be gone a half hour later. We wondered how this man was treating all these people. It was just amazing.[29]

Despite his skill and seemingly limitless energy, Burwinkel had more than he and Falkenberg could handle. Crowded together in tropical heat without adequate food and water and virtually no sanitation, the refugees had their share of medical issues. Dehydration and diarrhea were running rampant, brought on by a complete lack of sanitation. With overtaxed and often non-working toilets on board the ships, refugees relieved themselves where they stood or used communal buckets. Both *Kirk* and *Cook* sailors found it necessary to come alongside many of these ships and train their fire hoses on the decks besmeared with feces. Jacobs said that they could smell the ships while they were still hundreds of yards away.

Lt. Cdr. Ray Addicott, *Cook*'s XO, vividly remembered the squalor that greeted his ship as it moved among the fleet: "The people were almost on top of each other. You can imagine the conditions that existed. It was nasty. Our sanitation team would come in and hose down all the decks. A lot of people would spread their clothes out so we could also hose the clothes down."[30]

Cook's skipper, Cdr. Jerry McMurry, recalled the conditions on one of the Vietnamese landing craft: "The ship was loaded with what I estimated were four thousand people, and the decks were just running with urine. We used fire hoses to wash down those decks and then we tried to get enough freshwater aboard because it was hotter than hell during the day—up to 110."[31]

During his rounds Burwinkel observed people scooping up buckets of seawater from the fantails of their ships because the sterns were much lower to the water. Even with repeated warnings, he was unsuccessful in convincing them not to use the saltwater they hauled up because that source of water they used for washing was polluted.

"Saltwater showers and saltwater washes are no fun, but with the right amount of soap you could overcome the salt in the water. Unfortunately the heads and the scuppers of those ships discharged from the fantail so they were essentially dipping into contaminated fecal material in the water they were using to wash their faces and hands. I tried to convince the COs, or people in charge of the ships, to have them dip the water from the forecastle, but that was too high out of the water, and they weren't capable of lifting the heavy buckets to the deck."[32]

If diarrhea was a direct result of the lack of sanitation, conjunctivitis, also called "pinkeye," was even more of an epidemic. "I saw many cases of conjunctivitis caused by the unsanitary conditions and exposure to the sun," Burwinkel lamented.[33] With the combination of sunlight exposure and contaminated water, the highly contagious disease raged among the flotilla of ships.

Kirk's corpsman added, "I was very much afraid of that conjunctivitis spreading because it is a very, very, virulent illness. If you've ever had pinkeye, your eyes swell shut and you can't see. It's easily spread through your hands touching your eyes, touching a handle, touching another person. In fact, I was afraid that if I caught it, that would be the end of it."[34]

A mere four days into the voyage, Burwinkel exhausted his supply of antibiotic ophthalmic ointment to treat the scourge of pinkeye. He ran out of Kaopectate and Lomotil to stem the epidemic of diarrhea, which went unchecked on board many of the South Vietnamese vessels. He also used up all his other drugs and dressings. Two critically needed items were diapers and baby formula. Without emergency resupply, Doc Burwinkel and his helpers were out of business. Jacobs recalled the hospital corpsman plaintively telling him that he was completely out of medical supplies. And as only a CO could pursue a course of immediate action, Jacobs responded, "So I got on the telephone and put in a call."[35]

Kirk was still about 250 miles southwest of Subic Bay, but despite the medical supply crisis, help was soon on the way in a roundabout fashion. More than thirty-five years have dimmed recollections of what occurred next, but the following scenario probably occurred:

Since the task force flagship had already returned to Subic, Jacobs most likely called Armitage, who was then on board the South Vietnamese flagship HQ-3. Jacobs knew Armitage could use his considerable influence to expedite an emergency delivery of medical supplies. A radio message from Armitage, which was sent to the Pentagon via *Kirk's* radio, presumably was routed through the commander of Naval Forces, Philippines in Subic Bay. The message then went to the offices of the Joint Chiefs of Staff and secretary of defense to the attention of Erich von Marbod, principal deputy assistant secretary of defense. His staff immediately began calling Air Force officials to get the ball rolling.

Von Marbod recounted, "[I made] a phone call or two not to order these things to be done but just to say, 'What in hell is being done?' I was told by telephone somewhere, even before I was back at the Pentagon, that we would make some air drops of food and medicine. As far as I'm concerned, it was Armitage that caused the air drop."[36]

Regardless of who actually made the request, it was already being processed. The CO of Clark Air Force Base near Manila already knew about the dire situation. The base's CO had relayed the appeal halfway around the world to the Air Force's Rescue Coordination Center (RCC) at Scott Air Force Base, Illinois, the organization responsible for approving all such requests.

The RCC quickly approved *Kirk's* resupply mission and the authorization went back to Clark Air Force Base. The local RCC at Clark, in charge of all airborne missions in the region, then ordered the mission to proceed. The 31st Aerospace Rescue and Recovery Squadron stationed at Clark received the assignment.

Seated at a table in the RCC command post adjacent to the flight line, the dispatcher scrambled the duty aircraft commander and the senior enlisted man on his duty roster. Each of them in turn notified the rest of the crew. The aircraft commander, Capt. Rogers Hemphill, and his navigator then reported directly to the RCC command post at Clark for a mission briefing. Spread on a table was a chart of the South China Sea with *Kirk's* location already indicated.

Apprised as to *Kirk*'s distance from Clark, Hemphill determined fuel load and special cargo requirements. Pilot and navigator, both already wearing their flight suits, went directly to the aircraft to meet the rest of the crew and the loadmaster.

A square-nosed HC-130P transport, with strange protrusions erupting from its aluminum skin, sat on the tarmac. This plane was no ordinary four-engine transport. It had been configured as an extended-range, combat search-and-rescue version of the C-130 Hercules. One of its missions was to extend the range of combat search-and-rescue helicopters by providing air refueling. The aircraft was also equipped to drop pararescue specialist teams and small bundles by parachute. In this case they were going to drop two 250-pound sealed drums filled with dressings, anti-diarrheal medicine (Kaopectate and Lomotil), ophthalmic ointment, diapers, and baby formula, courtesy of Clark Air Force Base Hospital.

As Hemphill and his navigator went through the preflight checklist, the loadmaster rigged the two drums to hang from tracks affixed to the ceiling of the cargo department. The navigator would control the release of the drums. In short order the Hercules was airborne and heading southwest for its rendezvous with *Kirk*.

At approximately 10:40 a.m. on May 5, *Kirk* crewmen who were topside heard the four throaty turboprop engines of a low-flying C-130. The plane was not unexpected, having already radioed its intention to make a first pass to gauge sea conditions, establish the ship's position, and then make its drop on the second pass. Pilot and navigator duly noted the dead-calm sea. As the Hercules overflew *Kirk*'s bridge, Doyle thought the plane, with its odd nose, unusual projections, and no visible markings on its camouflage-painted fuselage, was a "spook"—a spy plane commandeered for this special mission.

The plane banked left and made a wide counterclockwise circle before beginning its final pass. Its tail ramp was already in the down position. The navigator had gotten them on target and now he would release the drums to roll down their tracks and out the tail ramp. *Kirk*'s motor whaleboat was already at the drop point some five hundred yards ahead and starboard of the ship. The three crewmen on board heard by radio that the plane was ready for the drops. Just before 11 a.m., the first of two drums rolled from its tracks out the HC-130's tail ramp, then a second drum—both suspended from parachutes. Five minutes later, the whaleboat crew wrestled both drums on board and headed back to the mother ship with their precious cargo, compliments of the U.S. Air Force.

Doc Burwinkel was back in business.

TEN

DESTINATION SUBIC BAY

THE FLOTILLA OF South Vietnamese ships and their American shepherds proceeded east toward Subic Bay. With the danger of a North Vietnamese attack diminishing with each passing mile, tension eased as *Kirk*'s gig and motor whaleboat shuttled back and forth through the fleet. The crew of the warship-turned-humanitarian-assistance ship delivered vitally needed food and water. HMC Steve Burwinkel held sick call, and engineers and machinist's mates repaired cranky engines and bilge pumps. Other American vessels—sister ship *Cook*, plus *Mobile, Vega, Tuscaloosa, Barbour County, Denver, Deliver, Abnaki, Flint,* and *Lipan*—also maneuvered around the formation providing engineering, medical, and logistical support.

Late Saturday afternoon, May 3, a familiar and unwelcome sight—the freighter *Tan Nam Viet*—appeared to starboard. She was barely moving, with a towline stretching to a nearby tugboat. The tug's engines were overheating and nearly out of fuel. Doyle was particularly exasperated since it was his crew that had recently labored so intensively to repair the merchant ship's engine. He learned in a radio conversation that the freighter's crew had forgotten all the lessons the Americans had taught them. Somehow *Tan Nam Viet*'s crew had fouled the ship's fuel with saltwater.

"Not only did they contaminate their fuel tank, but we discovered that they continued to run that huge engine on the badly contaminated fuel. They tried to burn seawater!" Chief Engineer Doyle remembered, still with a hint of annoyance.[1]

Once again Doyle sent Lt. (jg) John Pine and his men to the rescue on board the motor whaleboat. Accompanying them were XO Dick McKenna and HMC Steve Burwinkel carrying sorely needed medical supplies and food to *Tan Nam Viet*. Refugees, especially babies and young children, who had been camped out on deck were suffering from exposure, eye infections, and diarrhea. In addition, the ship's food supply was nearly exhausted. *Kirk's* men brought evaporated milk, cereal, canned blueberries, cases of beans, rice, canned tuna, and even frozen flounder and salmon. "They were just overjoyed to get it," Doyle related with great certainty.[2]

When Lt. (jg) John Pine and his men arrived on board, they found the Vietnamese "engineer's helper." Despite the fact that the man couldn't speak a word of English, together they pulled a cylinder head off the main engine, which was no small task. A single piston in the huge engine was the size of a galvanized garbage pail, measuring nearly two feet in diameter. In the next two hours, they installed a new exhaust valve, reinstalled the cylinder head, and re-torqued the cylinder head bolts. In the meantime the other engineers cleaned the seawater out of the engine fuel system and managed to get the engine running. *Tan Nam Viet* was under way once again. Pine and his men then returned to *Kirk*, but McKenna and Burwinkel decided to remain on board the merchant ship a while longer. The chief hospital corpsman still had to attend to patients' needs and ailments.

As *Kirk* and *Tan Nam Viet* steamed together, a minor drama developed. *Kirk* had pumped five thousand gallons of fuel on board the freighter's tug just in case its services might again be needed. No sooner had the tug been refueled than its captain, who was then on board *Kirk*, shouted to Captain Jacobs, who was on the bridge with Doyle. The tug captain insisted on learning their current position.

Doyle recalled what happened next: "I said to the captain, 'Now that he's got a lot of fuel onboard, he may try to split and leave that refugee ship behind.' So the captain got the interpreter and went down to the Vietnamese lieutenant in charge of the tug, and said, 'If you don't go back over to that ship, tie up to it, and take it into Subic, I will take my big 5-inch gun and shoot you!' That got that little Vietnamese tug captain all excited, and he quietly went back and tied up to the freighter."[3]

Just before 10 a.m., *Kirk* rendezvoused with *Tran Nhat Duat* (HQ-3), the flagship of the much diminished Vietnamese navy. As the warship pulled to starboard of HQ-3, which was a former U.S. Coast Guard cutter, *Kirk* threw lines over to the flagship. OS Jim Bongaard noted how unusual it was for two large vessels to "raft up" at sea. "[This was an] event that rarely happens in the Navy," Bongaard said. "Number one, you have to have perfectly calm seas. And number two, you don't just tie alongside another ship unless something's going on. It had never happened to me before."[4]

As the ships drew closer, the refugee situation became close and personal. With anguish in his voice, Bongaard continued, "I stepped outside and was just overwhelmed with emotion along with everybody else there. There were just thousands of people on top of this deck. And you're looking down at them. I had my camera so I took a few pictures and just had to stop taking pictures. I felt bad about taking pictures. I can't really describe the look on these people's faces. You see that same look on the faces of refugees in *National Geographic* and in documentaries. They have that look about them. They're fleeing—so in one way they're happy. But in another way, they don't know where they're going. It's sort of a blank, odd stare."[5]

MMFN Kent Chipman noted that the refugees "were just crammed in there just as tight as you could get. There were just thousands of people. . . . And they were sitting, standing. . . . They were just crammed on [that deck] just like with the Hueys and overloaded to the max."[6] Chief Burwinkel pondered, "If there were that many people we could see on deck, I figured below deck there had to be twice that number."[7]

The reason for the "house call" was HQ-3's urgent request for assistance. Her diesel generators were not functioning and the ship was out of freshwater. How safe that water was even before it ran out was questionable since many passengers were suffering from diarrhea. Three personnel from *Kirk*'s Engineering Department boarded the flagship to repair the generators while other crew members transferred four thousand gallons of freshwater from *Kirk*'s water tanks.[8]

Burwinkel dealt with several medical issues that day. One was the emergency medevac of the patient with a compound leg fracture. That transfer was made possible only after mechanics from *Kirk*'s LAMPS detachment built a workable helicopter from the fuselage of one Huey and the tail pylon of another. The other event was the arrival of Lan Tran, a young woman in her ninth month of pregnancy. Her mother accompanied the seventeen-year-old daughter seemingly about to give birth on the high seas.

The following day, Sunday, was anything but a day of rest on board *Kirk*. At 7:30 a.m. medical reinforcements arrived from the attack cargo ship USS *Mobile* (LKA-115)—a physician, Lt. R. Lindsey Lilly, and three hospital corpsmen to assist the ship's two overworked corpsmen. Chief Burwinkel welcomed the support. He had been shuttling among the formation attending to thousands of patients either in the motor whaleboat, captain's gig, or a commandeered swift boat while his assistant, HM3 Mark Falkenberg, held down the fort in *Kirk*'s sick bay. Burwinkel had just returned from his stay on board *Tan Nam Viet*, but he hadn't had a good night's sleep in days. The chief corpsman was running on adrenalin. USS *Abnaki* (ATF-96), an oceangoing tug, had loaned a corpsman for a few days and now came by to pick him up.

Abnaki's motor whaleboat was only one of many small boats that came and went throughout the day delivering supplies and several passengers. Besides providing personnel from their medical department, *Mobile* began delivering tons of rice via their mike boat (landing craft). *Kirk* mustered a working party to heave the rice bags on board.

A little before 10 a.m., another mike boat—from the fleet replenishment stores ship USS *Vega* (AF-59)—arrived with five tons of supplies and seven tons of rice, which were quickly loaded on board through *Kirk's* transom. By midafternoon USS *Barbour County* (LST-1195) weighed in when its mike boat came alongside and transferred additional supplies. *Kirk's* own little "fleet"—whaleboat, gig, and swift boat—scurried about the South Vietnamese flotilla delivering the donated food and other supplies to where they were most needed.

As had already been determined earlier at Con Son Island—and most recently with HQ-3—distributing freshwater was a priority. MM3 Bob Heym had by now earned the well-deserved nickname "Water King." He had kept *Kirk's* evaporators running full blast, not only to replenish the four thousand gallons unnecessarily pumped on board HQ-3 the day before but also to feed *Kirk's* thirsty boiler. For a while at least, her crew would have to put up with "water hours," that is, rationing.

Although that precious fluid was in short supply, ingenuity was not. Heym and several other sailors devised a method of delivering water. The ship's 5-inch ammunition came in metal containers. Emptied of their contents, the containers became large canteens, easily manhandled into small boats and distributed among the South Vietnamese vessels.

The fast-paced activity that Sunday continued with the arrival of four more pregnant women. They and their families joined Lan Tran and her mother in the converted lounge-turned-mini–maternity-ward. With the latest arrivals, Captain Jacobs began the "birth watch," each day looking in on the women and encouraging them to have their babies. The first infant, he hoped, would be named in honor of his ship. But wish as he might, none of the women gave birth during the voyage.

If the officers and enlisted men of *Kirk* would not witness the miracle of birth on board their vessel, soon enough they would contend with the tragedy of loss. When a listless and lethargic one-year-old Bao Le with pneumonia arrived with his mother that Sunday, Dr. Lilly from *Mobile* and HMC Steve Burwinkel worked diligently to save the child. They first bathed him with alcohol to bring his 106-degree temperature down, then went to work treating his lung inflammation with penicillin. Burwinkel recounted, with poignancy, the treatment and heartbreaking aftermath: "We figured out the pediatric dose of penicillin, and he was basically cured of pneumonia. But, unfortunately, in the act of feeding him, he coughed or somehow aspirated what his mother was feeding him and he died."[9]

The crew had been following little Bao Le's progress and rooting for his recovery almost hour by hour for the two days he had been on board. His death now seemed to throw everyone into a depression. McKenna approached Captain Jacobs with the idea of holding a formal military funeral for the child on the ship's fantail. Since only the mother and son had been brought on board, McKenna dispatched Doyle in the gig to retrieve the father and Bao's siblings from a South Vietnamese LST about a mile away.

The distraught father, Pierre Le, had already heard that his son had died but did not know the circumstances. He knew the baby was very ill with pneumonia when his wife and son had been transferred to *Kirk* a few days before. "It was a very touchy, uncomfortable situation," Doyle remembered. "He asked me if his wife knew, but I didn't know what to say to him."[10]

Just before Doyle boarded the gig, he had heard snatches of despairing news of what had happened to the child and that his death was probably accidental. "Yes, your wife knows, and she is very sad," Doyle awkwardly responded to the father's anguished query. "In broken English, he kept shaking his head and saying, 'When we left Saigon we were six, and now we are five. We are very sad.'"[11]

The short trip back to *Kirk* would give Doyle an opportunity to interact with Pierre Le and his three young daughters. He asked the father to tell his little girls not to be frightened by the booming noise the gig's engine would make. "He understood that [and] so he told the kids, and [they] looked around in anticipation," Doyle said. "You could see they were all waiting for something to happen. As soon as the gig with that screaming loud engine pulled away, the youngest girl began jumping up and down, laughing and clapping her hands! Then all the kids started laughing, even the 'kids' on the gig crew—me included. It relieved all the tension in the boat. All of a sudden, the little girls were on a roller coaster ride, and they loved it all the way back to the *Kirk*."[12]

Around 10 that night, May 6, the ship's officers, dressed in their formal whites, and sailors not on watch gathered on the fantail for the military service. "The burial at sea was a heart-wrenching thing," Doyle related, "knowing we were so close to saving the baby and then having him die. Chief Burwinkel was just distraught. It didn't affect the way he did his job but he was just distraught. It was the first burial at sea that I had seen and it affected all of us, the entire crew. The captain conducted the service in accordance with the time-honored regulations for burial at sea and it was very touching."[13]

AW3 Don Cox of the LAMPS detachment and his comrade, Mike Washington, were two of *Kirk*'s unofficial musicians. The sounds of their two trumpets often resonated across *Kirk*'s decks. "We played for our own enjoyment and to entertain anyone who would listen," Cox said. "We would serenade the crew by playing during underway replenishments and just any time the skipper wanted some entertainment to make the work go faster. I was now asked to play 'Taps' at the proper time when they consigned the baby's remains to the ocean. The family was there along with many of the other Vietnamese, and the funeral was a very dignified event. We performed the service in the most professional manner we could—not having done it before but following the directions of Captain Jacobs. And in playing 'Taps,' it really hit home what these people were going through."[14]

The infant's father, Pierre, emotionally called to mind: "It was a chilly night, even as it was in summertime. And I still remember there's a moon, too. And I see that there are many soldiers in a line up there. I don't know if I can call it a coffin or not. But, you know, it's the body of my son wrapped under two flags: the Vietnamese flag and the American flag."[15] The child's body, encased in a small, weighted wooden box and draped in honor, rested upon a board near one of the ship's rails. As Cox's last solemn trumpet notes drifted across the quiet moonlit water, two sailors tipped the board and little Bao Le slid into the sea.

Kimmy, one of Bao's sisters, was five at the time. Although her parents had told her of her brother's death, she recalled that she probably didn't grasp what "death" meant. But she certainly remembered the funeral and, from a little girl's perspective, its immediate aftermath. "When he went over the side, I remember running towards the edge of the boat, standing there, looking down, and wondering, 'How come no one is going to get him?'"[16] As Kimmy lingered at the rail, one of *Kirk*'s sailors scooped her up in his arms and carried her to another part of the ship where he tried to distract the bewildered child with a piece of candy.

Cox and the others went below decks after the solemn ceremony concluded. *Kirk*'s Vietnamese interpreter, Joseph Pham, tried to absorb the latest loss: "It's again another toll of the war because even though the boy almost reach freedom, he died. This was very tragic and very sad and I felt very sorry for the family."[17]

Cox noted the heartrending tone in Pham's simple summation of the cost of war. "I remember asking Joseph if there was anything we could do for him. He looked at me and said, 'No, you've done too much already.' It was all very touching and left an indelible mark in the life of a twenty-year-old sailor."[18]

As Doyle walked across the flight deck the following day, one of the little Le girls erupted from a group of refugees and came running toward him. "I crouched over a little bit since it looked like she was going to run right into me. She then leaped off the deck and jumped right into my arms. She wrapped her arms around my neck, and her legs around my waist, and began laughing, giggling, and jabbering in Vietnamese. The little girl recognized me from the rollercoaster boat ride. She was about two years old or a little older."[19]

As the child laughed and tugged on his beard, Doyle suddenly felt very homesick for his own children half a world away.

Despite the tragedy, the motley flotilla plodded steadily eastward across the South China Sea, a body of water not noted for its placidity. With each sunrise both landsmen and experienced seafarers among the vessels noted the uncharacteristic calm.

Lt. Bob Lemke recalled that "the sea was calm as a lake. It was very mild and that allowed us to work well with the ships. Some of the ships were not very seaworthy, and this [calm] allowed them to transit, and it also allowed the *Kirk* to continue to use its small boats in transferring people and material back and forth. It was a gift from God that we had such wonderful conditions."[20] Another benefit of the glassy-smooth sea was the virtual absence of seasickness among the refugees, a condition that would have further dehydrated the very young and elderly.

Captain Kiem Do, the Vietnamese navy's former deputy chief of staff for operations and the mastermind of the seaborne evacuation, had lost track of his family during the chaotic escape from Saigon. But he, too, was now a refugee. From his vantage on board HQ-17, Captain Do also noted the benevolent conditions: "I thought it was a miracle to have seven days with flat, flat seas. People were living openly on the decks, thousands of people—women, children, old people. If the seas were rough, it certainly would be a disaster."[21]

Even though the ocean's tranquility counted as a major blessing, the suffering on board the South Vietnamese vessels continued unabated. The collective misery of so many displaced people packed above and below decks was readily apparent to any observer. The physical and emotional torment of individual refugees, especially among the children, may not have been so evident.

Fifteen-year-old Anh Duong's long and twisting journey began on April 28, the day before Saigon fell. Like many of her contemporaries, she enjoyed school, loved learning, and had many close friends. Her home life centered around a warm and devoted family. But the war, which had been going on longer than Anh had been alive, affected their everyday life incessantly. Each day the sounds of war drew closer, accompanied by the inevitable anxiety and uncertainty.

With the dreaded enemy finally at the gates, Anh and her family quickly crowded onto a helicopter meant for ten passengers. The Huey, now crammed with nearly thirty men, women, and children, struggled to lift off and head out to sea. Whatever dear objects she treasured—a favorite doll, photos of friends and pets, a necklace—fit into a little bag, which she clutched to her young body. The Huey, piloted by her brother, eventually landed on HQ-505, a former World War II U.S. Navy LST. But Anh and her family did not remain on board very long. A number of crew members had left their families behind and were intent on returning to Saigon to retrieve them.

After pulling alongside the mobile repair ship *Vinh Long* (HQ-802), each member of the Duong family had to jump across to that larger ship. "That was a near calamity for my cousin," Anh related with apprehension, "who almost missed the jump because he jumped at the wrong moment and couldn't reach the other side. A miracle happened and he was able to hang on to something sticking out from the ship. His feet were inches away from being smashed. Someone was finally able to grab him."[22]

But then it was Anh's turn to make that daring leap from the LST. She recounted, "I was only fifteen at the time and pretty short, but somebody shouted 'Jump!' I immediately jumped—stretching, stretching—trying very hard to reach the other side. I also realized right away that I wasn't going to make it. As far as I stretched, my hand didn't touch anything on the other side. Somebody finally grabbed me. Eventually I saw my dad. That's when I broke into a cold sweat. I cried for hours after the whole thing was over with."[23]

Anh's family ended up on the repair ship's top deck where they were given ponchos and some plastic sheeting to protect them from the sun and rain. "My mother handed me a soldier's helmet filled with water," she recalled. "Since we had no cups, we had to drink water from it. I saw oil floating in it but was so thirsty I drank like crazy even knowing that I was also drinking oil with it. Although we had brought dried food with us, water was the real concern. I couldn't get enough but I was told no, we had to be considerate. There was an adequate supply of water but no one knew how long we would be at sea and what would happen. So they were cautious in handing it out so that no one would end up dying of thirst."[24]

The despairing teenager gazed out at the ocean as she contemplated the loss of everything she held dear. "At night, if it wasn't raining, we removed the ponchos that were protecting us and looked up at the beautiful night sky. It was so dark but when you looked up, you could see all those shining lights— all those stars. I remember thinking of Vietnam, thinking of the soldiers who were left behind, and all the folks who weren't as lucky as I was in getting out. The only thing we now had in common were those stars. If they looked up they would see the same stars I was looking at. Vietnam was then so far away from me."[25]

ELEVEN

DIPLOMATIC CRISIS

O N MONDAY, MAY 5, the two-columned flotilla slowly steamed onward toward Subic Bay. As her log recorded, *Kirk* continued "aiding evacuees embarked on these vessels."[1] Life on board the warship had settled into a daily routine. Since the LAMPS helicopter was inoperable and in the hangar, AW3 Cox's newly assigned duty was to look after the needs of the five mothers-to-be in the "maternity ward." "Because there were little kids there, I played with them," Cox recalled. "We'd sing songs and I taught English just to pass the time and give them something to do. We couldn't let the refugees run unescorted around the ship. So when any of the women were feeling too claustrophobic, or just needed to get away from the group for a few minutes, I would escort them up to the flight deck."[2]

With Joseph Pham interpreting, Lan Tran and her mother requested more time above decks. Captain Jacobs instructed Cox to take personal responsibility for the two women, look after their needs, and make them as comfortable as possible.

"I'd take her and her mother up above decks," Cox reminisced, "and sit with her. We would talk, she in Vietnamese and I in English. Neither one of us really knew what the other person was saying. More than anything, I think she just needed to get some sunlight and have someone to talk to. I could see in her face her fear, her loneliness, and feelings of loss from leaving her homeland."[3]

Somehow, the twenty-year-old sailor and the seventeen-year-old Lan managed to communicate, mostly using their hands. Lan reminded Cox of his young sister and he grew very protective, while at the same time always conscious that she was another man's wife. Lan's mother was always present as an escort when he accompanied her above deck. Lan grew to trust and depend on the young airman to the point that she eventually felt comfortable enough to request a special favor. With Pham as interpreter, Lan asked Cox if he would be godfather to her child.

Not familiar with the concept of godfather in Vietnamese culture, he inquired, "What does a godfather do?" Pham explained that being a godparent meant being present at the christening, at birthdays, and other life events. If anything happened to Lan and her husband, it would be Cox's responsibility to raise the child. "The only thing I could think was that I was a twenty-year-old single guy in the Navy," Cox recounted, "and this was something I was not capable of doing or of committing to do. So I declined the honor."[4]

Nevertheless, Cox wanted to remember the young woman and took several photographs of her alone and some with her mother. He then asked her to take a photo of him. The airman recalled those lighthearted moments: "[I stood] in my most manly pose in front of one of the Hueys. I wrote my name and squadron information on the back of the photograph, and she wrote her name on the back of her photograph. I kept the two of her and she kept the one of me."[5]

OSSN Todd Thedell, another designated caregiver, was assigned to look after a refugee family that was still on board *Kirk*. The father was a U.S. citizen and his wife was Vietnamese. "I understood that he was an important man, and I was told that the care for his family was a priority. So for the week we were steaming to the Philippines, I made sure they were comfortable and fed. I played games, read to the young children, and taught them some English. I also learned some Vietnamese and made friends with them."[6]

That Monday morning the formation was still about 340 miles west of Subic Bay and cruising at seven knots. Shortly before 8 a.m., Vice Admiral Chung Tan Cang, chief of naval operations of the Vietnamese navy, his deputy, Commodore Hoang Co Minh, and Richard Armitage arrived on board *Kirk*. They needed to confer with Captain Jacobs and Commo. Pete Roane, commander of Destroyer Squadron 23. The main item on the agenda was the impending arrival of the flotilla into Subic Bay late the following day.

Guidance from U.S. Naval Forces, Philippines, headquartered at Subic Bay, and from Washington had so far been sketchy as to arrangements for receiving the South Vietnamese vessels and refugees. Until specific instructions arrived, the conferees decided that the best course of action was to send U.S. personnel—officers and experienced enlisted men—on board each of the Vietnamese vessels in preparation for the arrival. They would act both as "liaison" officers to assist the South Vietnamese crews and, depending on circumstances, assume command of those ships. These personnel came from at least six U.S. ships in the formation, with thirty-nine from *Kirk* alone.

Those thirty-nine selected from *Kirk* would be embarked on board seventeen of the warships and two fishing trawlers tagging along in the formation. Armitage was already on board *Tran Nhat Duat* (HQ-3). Within thirty minutes of the South Vietnamese VIPs' departure, XO Dick McKenna and Captain Jacobs selected those *Kirk* personnel to be embarked. They were soon dispatched to their assigned vessels on board gig, motor whaleboat, and swift boat.

The complicated legal and diplomatic ramifications regarding the ships and refugees entering Subic Bay were becoming evident and causing concern. With the fall of Saigon, South Vietnam no longer existed. The ships of that nation, as Chief Engineer Hugh Doyle described them, were "like ships without a country." Although they still flew the Vietnamese flag and crewmen wore the uniform of the Vietnamese navy, they were all in limbo.

Despite the fact that Subic Bay Naval Base was under U.S. control by agreement, those in authority did not know how the Philippine government would react to the former Vietnamese navy ships entering its territorial waters—or what would become of the evacuees. In recent negotiations with U.S. diplomats, Ferdinand Marcos, president of the Philippines, had balked at accepting the growing flood of South Vietnamese refugees who had been arriving on his doorstep since the beginning of April 1975.

That night *Kirk* received a coded message marked "secret." Jacobs and McKenna read it with growing concern, trying to absorb its implications.

Meanwhile, *Kirk*'s embarked personnel were acclimating to their new assignments. Lt. (jg) Don Swain from the LAMPS detachment and SA Carl Richardson had been put on board *Van Kiep II* (HQ-14), a 184-foot escort patrol vessel, formerly USS *Amherst* (PCE[R]-853). Fortunately, the ship's Vietnamese captain, Lieutenant Thanh Pham, spoke English. He explained to the two Americans that nearly all the refugees on his vessel had come on board in haste and as strangers. But none of them, he added, had been screened to determine their status as either bona fide refugees or communist sympathizers. Pham escorted Swain to the bridge and told him to remain there until it was deemed safe for him to come down. The next morning, Swain left the bridge and mingled with the refugees.

"I didn't speak any Vietnamese but a few people spoke a little bit of English, so we were able to communicate pretty well," Swain recalled. "It was a very well-disciplined ship and the commanding officer was definitely the commanding officer. The refugees obeyed him and his crew when it came to the proper operation of the ship and where it went. I was impressed."[7] Swain was also surprised by the condition of the patrol craft's engine room, which housed, as he remembered, "a bunch of in-series diesel engines which were absolutely spotless. The engineers and the engineering staff were down there making sure the thing kept running."[8]

What he witnessed above on the refugee-choked deck contrasted sharply with the seemingly modern and efficient engine room: "It was my first experience with a ship that had the restroom facilities as cut-out holes on the stern."[9]

LAMPS pilot Lt. Rick Sautter was stationed on board *Ly Thuong Kiet* (HQ-16), the former Coast Guard cutter *Chincoteague*. Like his fellow LAMPS pilot, Swain, he was astonished by the professionalism of the ship's Vietnamese naval personnel. Sautter related, "The guns were perfectly oiled and in perfectly good working order. As we were steaming around and even as late as going into the Philippines, the sailors were maintaining that ship, chipping paint and doing what they could to have it in good shape."[10]

On board *Huong Giang* (HQ-404), a 200-foot LSM, Ens. Bruce Davidson encountered a medical crisis that required an emergency radio call back to *Kirk*. A five-year-old girl was apparently suffering from dehydration. Davidson described her as being very hot and flushed and shaking uncontrollably. Lt. R. Lindsey Lilly, the physician on loan from USS *Mobile*, was called to *Kirk*'s bridge to talk to the Vietnamese medic on board HQ-404. Lilly advised the medic to give the child fluids, administer salt and aspirin, and get her temperature under control by bathing her. But by this point, the physician's advice made no difference. While they conferred by radio, the child lost consciousness. Ten minutes later, Davidson sadly reported that she had died.

Despite the little girl's death, the mortality rate among the thousands of refugees was remarkably low. Doyle noted, "We've lost very few so far when you consider the conditions they are living in. The sanitary conditions are horrible, the food is not the best, and there isn't much of it."[11] Throughout the drama, beginning on April 28, Doyle had been faithfully recording each day's events with a cassette recorder. Afterward he sent the cassette tapes to his wife back home. The elation and triumph in the young lieutenant's voice can still be heard today as he described the role *Kirk* was playing in the mass rescue:

I don't know what you've been reading in the news. I don't know how much of a play this evacuation of the Vietnamese navy is getting. I guess we are playing just a small part when you consider how many refugees there are total—twenty-five or thirty thousand people. . . . The whole thing was kind of cool how we did it, though, grabbing the entire [South Vietnamese] navy out of the hands of the North Vietnamese. I heard there was a comment made by Radio Hanoi the other night about "an American destroyer who flagrantly stole the entire Vietnamese navy." If you saw that comment, that was USS *Kirk*! We were the ones who grabbed it![12]

If *Kirk* had indeed snatched the Vietnamese navy from under the nose of the enemy, what now was to be done with that navy? The secret message Jacobs and McKenna had just read with concern more than hinted that a serious diplomatic crisis had developed, a dilemma that threatened the entire plan—and the welfare of the refugees.

"South Vietnam had fallen and the Philippine government had already recognized the communist government as the lawful government of all of Vietnam," Doyle pointed out. "So the Vietnamese flag—the gold with the three horizontal red stripes—no longer had any meaning to the Philippine government. Of course, it had infinite meaning to the Vietnamese refugees who were willing to die for that flag."[13] Ferdinand Marcos informed the U.S. ambassador to the Philippines, William Sullivan, that since the Republic of Vietnam no longer existed, the South Vietnamese vessels and their refugees would not be allowed to enter Subic Bay or any other port in the Philippines.

But Marcos' decision to embarrass a close ally, and therefore put the U.S.-Philippines relationship in jeopardy, contained undercurrents of preserving his own country—and his continued personal rule. Marcos, it seemed, was torn between his alliance with the United States and a desire to become an integral part of a changing Southeast Asia. Indeed, he had made overtures to North Vietnam even before the collapse of the Saigon government. The Filipino dictator also perceived that the United States no longer seemed committed to or even capable of countering communist expansion in Southeast Asia. If the leader of the free world had abandoned South Vietnam, what guarantee did Marcos have that his nation would not be left in the lurch? The fall of South Vietnam had provided the strongest signal yet that the Philippines had to reevaluate its foreign policy in the face of new Asian associations. And the changing political landscape meant normalizing relations with communist governments in Cambodia, Laos, and Vietnam. This shifting Southeast Asia reality, as Marcos viewed it, trumped the historic relationship with the United States.

Marcos had not manufactured the current situation. The state of affairs had been thrust upon him by the tides of war. Since Hanoi had already requested the return of the "stolen" ships, permitting their entry into the Philippines risked offending the North Vietnamese. Unless and until American and Filipino negotiators could find a solution, the flotilla and its desperate human cargo would remain at sea.

Capt. Paul Jacobs and the other participating U.S. Navy COs faced their own dilemma. Conditions on board the Vietnamese vessels were steadily deteriorating despite their best efforts to supply food, water, and medical supplies. Many refugees had been at sea for more than a week. Some were demoralized by the demise of their nation and, in so many cases, by the death of family members. Others were despondent over having left spouses and children behind. More than a few were reaching the end of their rope. All faced an uncertain future.

Maintaining law and order on board some of the ships had been tenuous since the very beginning of the operation. COs recalled hearing reports of mutiny, rioting, and even firefights on board overcrowded transports that had fled South Vietnamese coastal cities as recently as two weeks before. And despite the best efforts to disarm the refugees, smuggled weapons lurked behind bulkheads and cable runs, beneath anchor chains and coils of line, and in other hiding places too numerous to count.

Stalling for time—while hoping the diplomats could work their magic—seemed the only immediate course of action. *Kirk* and the other escorts gradually slowed, and, as night approached, helmsmen were instructed to ease their wheels gradually to starboard, keeping in view the stern lights of the ships ahead. The escorts then began a series of course changes, turning away from the Philippine coast. The maneuver, carried out in darkness, would encompass a huge circular track, covering hundreds of square miles. The clockwise tactic would also eat up time and, they speculated, be imperceptible to the refugees. If passengers concluded that the ships were taking them back to Vietnam, the ensuing panic and chaos would be unimaginable.

"Would their hopes be dashed?" Doyle pondered. "Were they to be repatriated to their dreaded communist enemies? How could the officers in charge of this vast formation get reassuring word out in sufficient time to avoid massive unrest—even rioting—aboard these ships?"[14] Despite these concerns, the maneuver, which took almost an entire day to complete, succeeded "without alarming a single refugee," Doyle related.[15]

Thankfully the twenty-four-hour delaying tactic gave Ambassador Sullivan time to exercise his diplomatic skills. Perhaps no one was better suited to the task than the distinguished white-haired career diplomat who had played an integral role in negotiating the Paris Peace Accords two years before. Known as one of "Kissinger's boys," Sullivan had served in many foreign posts, his previous assignment as ambassador to Laos. He often acted independently with Secretary of State Kissinger's tacit approval.

According to his longtime friend and colleague Erich von Marbod, Sullivan had already cultivated a special relationship with Marcos and the Filipino people since he established himself as ambassador in Manila. Sullivan was perceived as both powerful and credible. He not only had the ear of Henry Kissinger but clearly spoke for the most authoritative secretary of state in recent memory, and that influence could not be underestimated. "If Bill Sullivan asked Marcos for something or told him what needed to be done," von Marbod pointed out, "Marcos would do it. He had clout!"[16]

Even before the South Vietnamese fleet began its voyage from Con Son Island, Sullivan and Marcos had discussed the South Vietnam "problem" in several meetings. The Philippine president told the diplomat that he would not admit more than 2,500 Vietnamese refugees into the Philippines. The imminent arrival into Subic Bay of the Vietnamese navy flotilla now created an emergency situation. According to Sullivan, those sensitive and personal negotiations took place during the annual ceremony commemorating the fall of Corregidor to the Japanese on May 6, 1942.

Following the customary speeches, Sullivan realized, as stated in his memoir, "I would have to speak with Marcos there on the platform if there was any urgent matter I needed to raise. And as of that morning, I did have an urgent problem."[17] The ambassador managed to detach Marcos from the others on the platform and quietly informed him of the unfolding developments. As Sullivan recounted in his chronicle, the Philippine president reminded the diplomat that the base agreement between the United States and the Philippines "permitted Subic to be used only by U.S. public vessels and that there was no sanction given to bringing Vietnamese naval units into the facility. He would have to stand by the terms of the agreement."

The quick-witted Sullivan immediately saw a possible solution to the dilemma—a provision of the Military Assistance Program, which had, in the first place, provided ships to the Vietnamese navy. If the receiving nation no longer had use for donated equipment—in this case, American-supplied ships—those ships could be returned to U.S. ownership. Marcos listened intently, then asked if title to those vessels could be transferred to the Philippines. "While such an eventuality was nothing I could promise," Sullivan stated, "I assured him that there was a logical consistency to that outcome."[18]

The ambassador assured Marcos that he would personally recommend the transfer of most of those vessels to the Philippines. The two men then shook hands and descended the platform. The provisions of their gentlemen's agreement would now be implemented. The South Vietnamese vessels would be turned over to U.S. command, and South Vietnamese flags would be replaced with American flags. The ships would then be disarmed and enter Subic Bay as U.S. Navy ships. As for the refugees, they could remain in the Philippines for just a few days until the United States arranged for their transportation elsewhere.

On Tuesday, May 6, word reached *Kirk* and the other U.S. Navy ships, outlining the course of action. Since American personnel were already on board the Vietnamese vessels, they would take command, be responsible for reflagging and disarming the ships, and then bringing them into port.

Satisfying all these conditions meant a very busy day and a half for *Kirk*'s embarked personnel and other crew members who joined them to assist with this unexpected assignment. The most difficult task was collecting thousands of small arms from the Vietnamese ships and transferring them to mike boats. Many were simply thrown into the ocean. Even more laborious was the disassembly of naval guns exceeding 5-inch- or 40-mm-bore diameter. Once disabled, the breech mechanisms were to be dropped over the side. South Vietnamese and American sailors then emptied magazines of their 20-mm, 40-mm, 81-mm, 3-inch, and 5-inch ammunition. Working under the intense tropical sun, they heaved all the ammo overboard.

But the most sensitive and emotional chore was the reflagging. Captain Jacobs and commanders of other U.S. ships present scrounged around for new and old flags from lockers and wherever else they could find them. Orders to *Kirk*'s embarked personnel were then dictated and printed. Packages containing both flags and orders were subsequently prepared for delivery to the Vietnamese navy ships. Lt. Bob Lemke, from Commodore Roane's staff, was ordered to deliver the packages to the Americans designated to take command.

"I was asked to deliver the orders to each of the ships, to each of the Americans on the ships," Lemke recalled, "and then to go to HQ-3, where I would deliver the flag. I would then go through the ceremony and be the American representative on that ship."[19] The orders he carried to each vessel were brief and concise: "From Commander Destroyer Squadron 23. You will assume United States Naval custody and command of the Republic of Vietnam ship _____ at a time specified by direction of Commander Destroyer Squadron 23 on 7 May 1975. Your immediate superior in command will be Commander Destroyer Squadron 23."[20]

On board the captain's gig, Lemke went from ship to ship delivering the orders and flags. As the gig pulled alongside each ship in turn, Lemke handed up the package enclosed in a manila envelope. Although the Vietnamese had been made aware of what was to occur, the atmosphere on board each vessel became tense and uneasy.

Captain Kiem Do sadly recollected the events: "A young officer came on board our ship and said, 'You'll have to lower the flag and hoist the American flag up and sail in.' I said to him, 'We lost our country. We lost our pride. We lost everything. But please, a last favor. Try to have a ceremony of down the flag and raise the flag up, a ceremony that would save us some face, particularly [for] those people aboard the ship, thousands of them.'"[21]

"We had a very emotional ceremony," Do continued. "All the people flocked to the deck and sang the national anthem, crying at the same time to lower their flag and then raise the American flag ceremoniously. So the dignity is there. Even though it is a big loss for us, at least it saved our face and also our dignity."[22] "It was kind of a feeling of finality," recalled Lt. Rick Sautter. "That was kind of the final step in the fact that South Vietnam no longer existed."[23]

On board HQ-3 Lemke watched a crew member take the American flag to the mast and announce over their 1MC system that the ceremony was about to begin. The ship was silent. No one spoke. It was absolutely quiet. Then, as a South Vietnamese officer prepared to lower the South Vietnamese flag, his crew sang a capella the national anthem of their former country. It was a very moving time. As the yellow and red colors were slowly brought down, the refugees joined the crew in singing their national anthem. All were caught up in the moment as to what the lowering of their flag symbolized—a country no more. "They sang, the flag was lowered, and then in silence the American flag was raised," Lemke remembered with much emotion. "And we continued in silence for quite some time."[24]

Dam Thuy Nguyen poignantly summoned up her own experience on board her refugee ship: "It was our tradition in our country to sing the national anthem and salute the flag. We just did it. We never really thought deeply about its meaning. But now a rush of patriotic fervor swept over me. I looked up at the flag as they slowly lowered it and cried like a baby. I realized that I would never see my flag again. We realized that it meant we were losing our land. That flag represented the country where I was born. It was a big loss. We were now family-less, country-less. It was all gone."[25]

On board another transport, HQ-16, Sautter ensured that their ceremony would be done with as much dignity as possible. Observing the solemn reflagging ceremony, he noted a feeling of resignation. "That was kind of the final step in the fact that South Vietnam no longer existed."[26]

Lieutenant Thanh Pham, CO of HQ-14, was at first confused by what was to occur. He asked Swain to explain why the ships were to be reflagged and turned over to the Americans. Swain said he didn't know why but informed the CO, "The Philippine government was acting like governments do and we're gonna do what we have to do to get all you guys into a safe port."[27] Pham then announced to the refugees on board HQ-14 that the Vietnamese flag would have to come down and asked everyone to stand by and prepare for the ceremony. A sailor then lowered the flag and raised the American flag in its place. "That flag symbolized freedom and what we had been fighting for generations," Pham's brother-in-law, Liem Bui, remembered. "At that moment we believed we lost everything. I saw that everyone's eyes were teary, even my dad and myself. That was a very strong emotion. We had fought for freedom but in the end it happened like this."[28]

"It was very, very sad," Pham recounted. "We cried, but no one could see tears in our eyes. We cried in our hearts. When we left Vietnam, I looked at my ship's flag and realized that this flag no longer flew over our land in South Vietnam. Only my ship and others in the same group [had] still kept this flag flying freely. We lost our country. We lost everything. During the ceremony all people, both civilian and military, stood on the deck. We saluted our flag and then the American flag was hoisted. All our men then took off their shoulder boards and threw them into the sea."[29]

When the brief ceremony concluded, Pham walked over to Swain and offered him the bridge. Taken aback by the gesture, the American officer responded to the CO's request, "I'm a naval aviator. I don't drive boats. I drive aircraft. You're an American now. Drive the boat and follow those ships in front of you." Still reeling from Pham's offer to take over command, Swain clearly remembered, "And that's exactly what he did."[30]

Thirty-two ships, again part of the U.S. Navy, prepared to enter Subic Bay.

At 12:27 p.m. on Wednesday, May 7, *Kirk*'s log recorded a Filipino aircraft flying over to check the man-of-war's identification. Two hours later *Kirk* passed Grande Island in Subic Bay just under a mile to starboard.

AW3 Don Cox noted a sudden change of mood among the refugees on board *Kirk*. "As they saw us coming into Subic Bay, there was an elation that went through the refugees that they finally were safe and that they had a new life ahead of them. And the new life was going to be much better than anything they could have imagined under communist rule. And there were a lot of smiles, a lot of smiles by then."[31] At 3 p.m. *Kirk* moored at Wharf West, portside to USS *Benjamin Stoddert* (DDG-22) in Subic Bay, Republic of the Philippines. The warship had ended her five-day, thousand-mile humanitarian odyssey across the South China Sea.

In the meantime the other South Vietnamese ships had been instructed to anchor in the bay. Three were moved to a pier where the refugees were off-loaded; then they immediately were herded on board Military Sealift Command ships for transportation to Guam. The others spent two nights in a temporary refugee camp set up on Grande Island. As per the terms of the diplomatic agreement, these refugees boarded vessels either operated or contracted by the Military Sealift Command and were on their way to Guam within two days.

But not all went smoothly. On board HQ-14, Swain heard rumors circulating ashore that the refugees still on board ship were in a foul mood and could riot at any moment. Marines and security personnel therefore prepared to storm the ships to deal with the unrest. "I had a bunch of Marines start jumping aboard my ship and I had to stop them," Swain recounted. "I explained to them that these were great people. There was nothing going on, and if they were there to secure the ship, that was fine. But there was nothing to panic about and that they should stay calm. Everything would turn out all right." But Swain added in relief, "A Marine told me that he was there to escort me off the ship and take me into port. That was fine with me. I then said goodbye to everybody and went with him in a small boat to the pier."[32]

Kirk's other embarked personnel remained on board their respective ships until they were relieved by U.S. Navy Ship Repair Facility personnel and taken ashore by small boats. All were back on board *Kirk* by midnight, physically and emotionally drained, but relieved to be among their shipmates once again.

EPILOGUE

JUST PAST MIDNIGHT on Thursday, May 8, 1975, USS *Kirk* lay at Subic Bay's Wharf West pier. She was on dock power now and the men no longer had to contend with water hours. Nevertheless, the normally shipshape vessel looked as though she had either confronted a typhoon or had hosted the ultimate fraternity party. To be sure, *Kirk* had "entertained" hundreds of refugees, and the ship therefore needed more than a cursory cleaning. Her larder was nearly empty. At the very least, before she would be again ready for sea duty, her food stores and other supplies had to be replenished. Some of the maintenance crew thought she required time in the yard for an overhaul.

The condition of the flight deck may have added to that assessment. Three trophy Hueys she had brought into port still had to be craned ashore, not to mention her own LAMPS helo, which called for a long-awaited engine replacement. Beneath their skids, the flight deck was in sorry shape. Because the deck's nonskid surface was so gouged and abraded by the many Hueys that had been dragged to their watery deaths, it would need a complete resurfacing. On their way to being thrown overboard, the helos had banged against the ship's steel hull, causing scrapes and abrasions on her sides. But these pits and dents were simply cosmetic imperfections that a new coat of gray paint would easily remedy.

And the condition of her crew? Those still awake that early Thursday morning grabbed "midrats" (midnight rations) in the crew's mess and traded stories with the men who had just returned from duty on board the Vietnamese ships, several of which still lay at anchor in the bay. Exhausted as they were by the previous week's drama at sea, many found sleep impossible. Although the implications of their mission would not be apparent for some time, more than a few already suspected that they and their beloved *Kirk* had just carried out a seemingly mission impossible. Some crew members, however, merely shrugged off the past week's rescue as nothing more than an "unusual" bump in what was a routine WESTPAC deployment.

The mission had ended for the men of *Kirk*, but what would happen next for the refugees? They had been brought out of harm's way, but their future was a blank page. As HMC Steve Burwinkel observed, "After all, we were going home. We had a home to go to. They had just left their home and didn't know what was facing them in the future."[1] The next phase on the long journey for the former citizens of South Vietnam was about to begin.

Even as Operation Frequent Wind—the helicopter evacuation of Saigon—had been under way, Operation New Life, activated the first week of April 1975, continued. This evacuation, which was to last for many months, removed an estimated 112,000 Vietnamese refugees from South Vietnam. Approximately 94,000 would find permanent homes in the United States. Most would first end up in hastily assembled refugee camps on Guam, and then as residents at the Marine Corps base at Camp Pendleton, California; Fort Chaffee, Arkansas; Eglin Air Force Base, Florida; and Fort Indiantown Gap, Pennsylvania. They would remain in these camps while awaiting sponsors. Each refugee's passage to freedom was unique.

Joseph Pham, *Kirk*'s indefatigable translator, left the moored *Kirk* and accompanied the five pregnant women to Naval Hospital Subic Bay. Each near-term woman quickly received a thorough examination. Following a good night's rest, all were escorted back to the docks where they boarded a transport ship chartered by the Military Sealift Command. After brief stops at Wake and Midway, the vessel arrived at Guam. The refugees were then taken to the tent city at Orote Point, once the site of an active airstrip.

"It was a mixed feeling," Pham emotionally called to mind. "We were glad to reach the freedom we were seeking, but we were also sad that from that time on we would no longer be able to return to our country and all the people we left behind."[2] After being assigned to a tent with his family, Pham's son came down with measles and began running a high fever. The following day the family was relocated to bachelor enlisted quarters, while his child received attention in the nearby tent hospital—care that included a remedy he had not seen back in Vietnam. "They put ice on him and his temperature went down very quickly," Pham remembered. "In fact, his body turned purple because of the cold. That was the first time we had ever encountered that treatment for the measles."[3]

Less than ten days after leaving Subic Bay, Pham's wife went into labor. That day, May 18, she gave birth to a daughter at the Naval Regional Medical Center. Several days later, Lan Tran's baby was born in the same hospital.

From Orote Point, the Phams moved to Guam's Camp Asan, where they remained until the middle of June, when the camp closed. Their next passage wound through Hawaii, and then on to the large and well-organized refugee settlement at Camp Pendleton, California. "Every refugee family registered for a sponsor, and they tried to match sponsors with refugee families," Pham recounted. "They matched us up with a sponsor named John Murphy, who happened to be historian for the U.S. Marines."[4]

After only four days at Camp Pendleton, Pham and his family flew to Fort Worth, Texas, to join the Murphys. They lived with the Murphy family for several months before moving to a small apartment near that city. In Fort Worth, Pham obtained a part-time job teaching English to immigrants for $7 an hour. Good luck shone on the Phams. Pham's sister and her family, who had escaped South Vietnam just a few days before they did, located her brother through the Red Cross. "So in early 1976, we relocated from Texas to the Northwest. And we've lived here ever since," Pham related.[5]

Pham attended school to learn graphics and then worked in the graphics industry for a few years. At the same time he taught ESL (English as a Second Language) to young children of Vietnamese immigrants in the Seattle area. Several jobs later, he went to work as a court reporter, a job he has held ever since. Eventually his sisters and mother left Vietnam and were reunited with the rest of the family.

"I count myself among the lucky few. So that's why I try to get any opportunity to return the favor to my community because of my deep sense of gratitude to the people who saved us. This is especially true of the *Kirk* people and all those who saved our lives and brought us to freedom."[6]

Dam Thuy Nguyen's passage to freedom continued from Subic Bay on board a Military Sealift Command transport to Guam. Still accompanying her was her nephew who had escaped from Saigon with her. When they arrived on Guam, like the Phams, they were assigned a tent at Orote Point, which they shared with a family of four. Compared to their life of privilege in Saigon, the daily routine now meant standing in long lines for meals.

"The line kept moving among the dust and sun. It was very hot and dirty but we had no choice," Nguyen said, still remembering those days of distress.[7] Food in the camp was served on thin paper plates. She and her nephew both agreed to get just one meal for both so they could use the other plate to protect the food from the ever-present dust. "They put one scoop per person of wet rice on the plate like ice cream. And, because they thought that Asian people liked fish," Nguyen recalled with a smile, "there was also fish but it was so fishy. I had to use Tabasco or something to make it red and spicy. Then we went up to the hill near a tree and shared and ate that one scoop of rice and the piece of fishy fish."[8]

After three weeks on Guam, Nguyen and her nephew flew to Pennsylvania and took up residence at the Fort Indiantown Gap refugee camp near Harrisburg. The camp was a vast improvement over what they had experienced on Guam. They had real beds, showers, ample food, and, above all, some mobility. A bus system ran through the camp, enabling them to visit new friends and the Red Cross office. Eventually Nguyen's aunt, who lived in Paris, was able to contact another cousin in Fort Worth, who found a sponsor for her and her nephew in Texas. When she learned they would be going to "cowboy country," also known as "Texas," Nguyen grew apprehensive.

"When we were back home, we watched cowboy movies. And they all wore hats, boots, and rode horses. My nephew asked me, 'I'm small. How can I climb or jump onto a horse?' We were both so worried about the new life. How would we be able to adapt to that life? We looked at each other and both laughed and cried."[9]

When their plane landed in Fort Worth, Nguyen saw cars parking at the airport. "I turned to my nephew and screamed like a crazy woman, 'Look, they have cars!' I was so happy!"[10] The sponsor family had already rented an apartment for them. Her nephew went to school but each day she wondered how they would survive.

Desperately needing a job, despite being an experienced teacher, she was ready, she said, to "be a cleaner or anything. I would do whatever it took to survive." Finally, after months of trying to find work, and using her considerable powers of persuasion, Nguyen got a job teaching GED students. She also sold Avon products in the evenings and on weekends. She was at last able to support herself and send money to family members she had left back in Vietnam. Eventually she sponsored them to come to the United States.

After being an instructor in Texas for more than two years, she accepted a teaching position in Michigan. She worked at this job until moving east to teach at an adult education center in Arlington, Virginia. Six months later the YMCA offered her a position as director of refugee services for metropolitan Washington, D.C., managing a program that sponsored refugees from Ethiopia, Angola, Afghanistan, Laos, Cambodia, and Vietnam.

In 1989 Nguyen spoke at a ceremony honoring her as one of *Washingtonian* magazine's "Washingtonians of the Year." "Vietnam and America. I love them both," she proudly declared. "I was born in Vietnam and was reborn in this country."[11] Nguyen has since married retired Army major general Victor Hugo Jr. Her faithful nephew, who shared the long and perilous journey from Saigon to America—and whom Nguyen would not abandon—became a chemist, got married, and has two children.

When she remembers the country she left behind, Nguyen reaffirms her feelings for the nation she has adopted as her own, asserting, "Now this is my land. I love it and I will die here."[12]

Lan Tran spent her one and only night in Subic Bay at the naval hospital with the other pregnant women. Due at any time yet fearful she would be left behind, she was adamant about leaving with the others. The next day, Lan and her mother boarded a Military Sealift Command transport to Guam. The crowded conditions, very unlike what she had enjoyed on board *Kirh*, sapped her appetite. "I remember they give everybody one box of food with a military ration—cigarettes and fruit cocktail. I give it away to other people. I just get one can of fruit cocktail, that's all."[13]

When the ship arrived at Guam, Lan was immediately taken to the Naval Regional Medical Center. That same night she gave birth to her daughter. Remembering Captain Jacobs' wishes about naming the first baby born on the ship after *Kirk*, she was perplexed. "Because I have a baby girl, I cannot put 'Kirk' as her first name. So her middle name is 'Kirk,'" Lan proudly pointed out.[14] The young mother's three-day stay in the hospital was interrupted by a visitor; none other than Captain Jacobs came to see her and the infant named for his ship.

Ten days later Lan, her mother, and her newborn flew to Camp Pendleton. Three months later she learned from Red Cross officials that they had located her missing husband at the camp in Fort Chaffee, Arkansas, where he had desperately been trying to find her. He had gone to the Red Cross office at Fort Chaffee every day to see if Lan's name was posted on the bulletin board. When he was unable to find her name, he began losing hope. He later told her that the other pilots had been able to leave with their wives, but by following military orders, he remained behind longer than he should have. He was then tormented by guilt for not taking care of his young, expectant wife.

After they were reunited at Camp Pendleton, the Tran family remained at the base for another three months until a Baltimore church offered to sponsor the Trans and bring them to Maryland. In September 1975 Lan, her husband, and baby—joined by his parents, sister, and brother—moved east and lived in Baltimore. As she pointed out, it is customary in the Vietnamese culture for the wife to stay with her husband's family; her mother had gone on to Canada, where her sister was living.

Shortly after arriving in Baltimore, her husband, who spoke English, found a job in an optician's office making glasses. After only a month of church-sponsored assistance, the Tran family could pay their own rent and support themselves. The church continued to cover their health-care expenses. After nine months in Baltimore, the family moved to California to join other relatives.

"It was so cold in Maryland we couldn't stand it so that's why we left there," Lan recalled.[15] With the proceeds from the sale of their car, they had just enough money to buy airline tickets for Lan, her husband, his parents, and his brother and two sisters. Several days after arriving in California, her husband landed a job. He worked while she went to school. Later he also attended school and learned enough about the graphics field to get a job at an advertising company. He died in 2001, leaving behind his wife, daughter Tien, and son James, born in 1977.

Lan's memories of her escape and subsequent rescue are still vivid, and her deep appreciation translated into a lasting and tangible form of gratitude. "I will never forget the experience on USS *Kirk* and the crew members who have extended their hand to helping us during our time of need. That's why I wanted to add 'Kirk' as my daughter's middle name."[16]

Lieutenant Thanh Pham, the former CO of escort patrol boat *Van Kiep II* (HQ-14), similarly began his serpentine journey to America. On May 8 he had brought his ship alongside a pier at Grande Island in Subic Bay. Everyone disembarked except for Pham and his family. American intelligence officers had come on board to question him about what he had observed when on a recent patrol near the Spratly Islands.[17] China, South Vietnam, the Philippines, and Taiwan had claimed ownership of the Spratlys, and Chinese warships had engaged South Vietnamese patrol vessels with gunfire.

Following the interview Pham and his family left the ship, which had already been secured by a party of U.S. Marines. "One Marine on duty saluted me and I saluted him back," Pham recounted. "I knew that this was the last time I could say good-bye to my dear ship."[18] The Phams went ashore, where they were provided with canned food and drinks. They then boarded a transport ship and at midnight began their voyage to Guam via the San Bernardino Strait in the Philippines. "On this ship," he remembered, "we slept on the upper deck and were provided C-rations for lunch and rice and fish for dinner. This was the first big dinner we had since the beginning of our long journey."[19]

The ship arrived at Guam on May 13, and the Phams, as with the other refugees, were assigned a tent at the Orote Point camp. A month later they were on their way to Fort Indiantown Gap, Pennsylvania. He recalled that after a number of flights "we took a bus from the airport to Fort Indiantown Gap. On our way, we were welcomed by many people when the bus passed by small towns. Many stood along the road and waved at us. They were welcoming us to America, and it made us feel good about American people."[20]

The Phams found the camp clean, near, and well managed. They lived in a one-hundred-person barracks, and everyone was responsible for keeping it clean. The camp administrators provided the refugees with ample food, entertainment, and health care. Pham was selected as a barracks chief and volunteered to work as a translator in the camp hospital. Although they were confined to the camp, eventually everyone in their barracks obtained sponsors and settled in different cities. When Pham and his family left Fort Indiantown Gap, one of the camp's area coordinators gave him a very positive letter of appreciation that he found useful to have later, when he applied for a job.

Their ticket out of the camp arrived that fall of 1975 under the sponsorship of Catholic Charities USA. The Phams would be moving to Wilkes-Barre, Pennsylvania. Their sponsor assigned them a volunteer student to help them get acclimated. Pham recalled their first meeting with Denise Goodwin: "When we arrived in Wilkes-Barre by bus, she was there with a French dictionary in her hand just in case. She was relieved and put her dictionary away when she realized that most of us spoke English—a broken English—but we could communicate. She was a wonderful young lady who helped us doing everything to prepare for our new life and eventually became our friend."[21]

The Phams moved into the apartment Catholic Charities had rented for them. They were soon joined by Pham's family, his wife's parents, and her brother's family. They all lived in the apartment for more than a year before moving to a bigger place. Pham soon found work as a cabinetmaker, then attended Wilkes College. He graduated in 1980 with a degree in electrical engineering. His first postgraduate job was as a field engineer for a Long Island company specializing in navigational systems. "During this time, I had the chance to work a couple of weeks on the Navy aircraft carriers *Coral Sea* and *Constellation*, and frequently I traveled to many Navy bases in the U.S. and an Air Force base in Canada."[22]

After working as a software designer for a large company in Annapolis, Maryland, Pham retired temporarily in 2006. But he began working again as a software designer for a health-care management firm in Annapolis. Like fellow refugees of the former South Vietnam, Pham and his family had come a long way since that sad day on board HQ-14 in May 1975, when they tearfully watched the flag of their vanquished nation hauled down for the last time. Through grit, hard work, and faith in their adopted homeland, these former homeless refugees earned their rightful place as Americans.

For the officers and men of USS *Kirk*, those events of nearly forty years ago, as well as their role in rescuing the South Vietnamese refugees, have had a profound impact. After several *Kirk* reunions at which rescuers met rescuees and where old friendships were renewed, perspectives have changed. The men of *Kirk* went to Vietnam as young men trained as warriors with an expectation of seeing combat. But when they neared the South Vietnamese coast, as Don Cox observed, they found that combat wasn't the order of the day.

"It was a heart and hand that was needed. We didn't recognize it at first. We just did our jobs. It was after that that we realized that our Vietnam experience was totally different from our brothers' who had walked in the field in combat. We recognized that it was going to be a positive experience for the rest of our lives. We were there to save life and not to destroy it."[23]

Bob Lemke, then on board *Kirk* as a member of Destroyer Squadron 23, has also recognized the extraordinary accomplishment of his shipmates who were called upon to take on a mission few could have imagined. "They were up to the task. They were American sailors ready to follow their leaders and do the best they could with what they had. They took their destroyer escort and made it a humanitarian service vessel, and they did an outstanding job."[24]

Hugh Doyle, *Kirk's* former chief engineer, remembered his shipmates' selflessness with a pride that has grown with the passing years. "The entire crew turned out and there wasn't a grumble or complaint among the crew. In fact, some of the crew emptied their lockers of their clothing, gave away all their candy that they [had] stored away for weeks. It was an amazing thing the crew did. It really was."[25]

OSSN Todd Thedell recounted his own small role in caring for the refugees: "I am not sure I have ever worked so hard with such a great bunch of people. I have always fondly remembered that week when I was an important person in someone's life."[26]

Kirk's "Water King," Bob Heym, put the experience into his personal timeline. "Of all the things I've done in my life, this is one of the things I'm most proud of. Real wealth comes from good memories. At the time, I had no idea that many years on I'd still be looking at that time. It makes me smile every time I think about it, even though I know that for the Vietnamese it was not a time for smiling. But I'm not smiling from glee. It's for knowing that something I did really counted."[27]

Doc Steve Burwinkel, idolized by the crew for his medical skills and compassion toward them, eagerly returned that affection. "The crew responded tremendously. I couldn't be more proud of a group of gentlemen. And I think they took great pride in helping these people when they realized the situation they were in."[28]

Richard Armitage, the brains of the successful rescue who witnessed first-hand the events of April–May 1975, had his own observations: "Seeing the men—and it was only men then—of the USS *Kirk*, and realizing how much a part of their lives and what a great capstone this was to their careers, moved me, [and] that they could feel so good about their involvement in that rescue. I envied them. They weren't burdened with the former misadventure of Vietnam."[29]

The *Kirk* story—for all its drama and emotion—endures because of its powerful human component and what it says about caring and compassion. At a *Kirk* gathering in Orlando, Florida, in 2005, Cox, the once twenty-year-old sailor who had taken a frightened and bewildered seventeen-year-old mother-to-be under his wing, had his reunion with Lan Tran, now the poised and elegant mother of two young adults. "Lan had been looking for me. I was her sailor and she and her mother were very tender in my heart. We had been reunited on the phone through the efforts of Jim Bongaard and the skipper.

We had talked and exchanged some photographs so we knew a little about each other and our history in the last thirty years."[30]

Kirk's former airman-turned-caretaker then continued in an animated tone, "I was in the hotel lobby checking in with my wife, Jackie, who herself anxiously looked forward to the event. Suddenly, out of the elevator came Captain Jacobs and Lan and her two children, Tien and James. Immediately Jackie got my attention and pointed. It was a very sweet reunion with a lot of wet tears."[31]

POSTSCRIPT

SINCE THE RELEASE of the documentary *The Lucky Few* in the fall of 2010, the *Kirk* story has generated much attention throughout the country. Some of that exposure was no doubt due to National Public Radio's coverage.[1] Since the NPR stories have aired, crew members have been reunited, and former refugees have reconnected to one another as well as bonded once again with some of their *Kirk* rescuers.

Following one of the NPR broadcasts, Capt. Paul Jacobs received a call from a woman in Texas who identified herself as Kimmy Le, the older sister of Bao Le, the one-year-old infant who had died on board *Kirk* and was formally buried at sea. A neighbor who had listened to the story on NPR called the father, Pierre Le, and told him what he had just heard. The young boy described in the story appeared to be Le's son. Indeed, the child was Bao Le. Le called his daughter, who then phoned NPR, and NPR relayed Jacobs' telephone number to Kimmy. A tearful conversation immediately followed.

At an October 2010 showing of *The Lucky Few* in the IMAX Naval Aviation Memorial Theatre in Pensacola, Florida, the Le family finally had their reunion with Steve Burwinkel, the hospital corpsman who had tried so valiantly to save their little son thirty-five years earlier. Prior to the showing, Captain Jacobs read a proclamation making the late Bao Le an honorary member of USS *Kirk*'s crew.

Other dramatic coincidences keep emerging—even decades later. Hugh Doyle, *Kirk*'s former chief engineer, lives near Newport, Rhode Island; as a retired Navy veteran, he receives his medical care from the Naval Health Clinic at the Newport Naval Station. When he recently went to the clinic for a checkup, he learned that his regular Navy physician had been reassigned and that a new physician, Lt. Cdr. Khan Van Nguyen, would be his new primary care doctor. At his first appointment Doyle asked his new physician when and how he and his family left Vietnam; he surmised that they may have been "boat people," a second wave of refugees who fled Vietnam in the late 1970s and early 1980s.

Nguyen responded that he really didn't know about the family's exodus since he was a baby at the time. Moreover, his father had since died without ever relating the story to him. Doyle gave the doctor a copy of *The Lucky Few* DVD, which Nguyen watched with his wife. Although Nguyen related to Doyle that he was moved by the film, he was none the wiser about his own history.

Dr. Nguyen's large family had settled in the San Francisco Bay area and flourished. Khan, the youngest of five children, recalled that his family never discussed their flight from Vietnam. After he watched the documentary, Khan talked intermittently with his mother and siblings, asking them more probing questions. The only information he could gather at the time was that they left Saigon on a large Vietnamese navy ship. His sister insisted that she remembered it had a large "1" painted on the hull. She also recalled that the ship went to an island and joined up with other ships heading for the Philippines.

Dr. Nguyen's sister and brother-in-law visited with him during a trip east to enroll their daughter at Boston College. During that stopover Khan showed them *The Lucky Few* and described their awed reaction: "They were blown away!" Since that time, Dr. Nguyen has been able to determine that his family escaped on HQ-1, which was part of a larger formation. His sister, who was a young teenager at the time, clearly remembered the re-flagging ceremony and *Kirk's* motor whaleboat coming alongside HQ-1 to deliver food, water, and medicine. Dr. Nguyen told Doyle that the film was an incredibly emotional experience for his sister and that the memories came flooding back to her.

Shortly after learning how the film had psychologically impacted Dr. Nguyen's family, Doyle hosted a public showing of *The Lucky Few* at his church's parish center. He introduced Dr. Nguyen, who, he had since learned, was not only a member of the same church but was a one-year-old boy on one of the ships (*Tran Hung Dao* [HQ-1]) in the documentary!

"What are the odds," Doyle asked in utter astonishment, "that that one-year-old boy would survive the war, escape from Vietnam with his family, come to the United States, attend medical school, join the Navy, be stationed at the Newport Naval Station, and become my doctor?"

THE LUCKY FEW AND OFFICERS
AND CREW OF USS *KIRK*

D
AVID ANDROSKAUT, Capt. John Bowman's copilot, was killed in an aircraft accident in 1978.

Richard Armitage has held many government positions since the Vietnam War ended, including deputy assistant secretary of defense, assistant secretary of defense, and deputy secretary of state. He is currently president of Armitage International in Arlington, Virginia.

James Bongaard left the Navy in 1975 and worked as a computer service technician for a number of years before retiring. In 2004 he founded the USS *Kirk* Association (http://www.kirk1087.org). He makes his home in Charlotte, North Carolina.

John Bowman retired as a lieutenant colonel in 1991 after more than twenty-five years with the Marine Corps. He worked as a contractor for NASA at the Goddard Space Flight Center in Maryland and now volunteers with the Wounded Warrior Mentor Program, advising wounded Marines and offering career counseling. He is also a volunteer at the Smithsonian's Udvar-Hazy National Air and Space Museum annex at Washington Dulles International Airport in Chantilly, Virginia, which is near his home in McLean, Virginia.

Stephen Burwinkel spent thirty years in the Navy, retiring in 1989. Since that time he has worked for the Civilian Health and Medical Program of the Uniformed Services (CHAMPUS) and Humana. He resides in Pensacola, Florida.

Kent Chipman, after leaving the Navy, worked for the city of Lake Charles, Louisiana. He is currently employed as utility plant supervisor (water purification) for the city of Longview, Texas.

Donald Cox, after duty with the Navy, attended college and earned a PhD. He now works as an engineering program manager in the defense industry in Tucson, Arizona.

Kiem Do settled in the United States, taught high school math and science, and also worked as a cost engineer with a Louisiana utility company before he retired in 1997. He is a resident of Mandeville, Louisiana.

Hugh Doyle, after his assignment on board *Kirk*, served as XO of USS *Fanning* (FF-1076) and retired from the Navy in 1987. He then worked for a management consulting firm before becoming a management consultant for the Derecktor Shipyards and retired in 1993. He makes his home in Middletown, Rhode Island.

Anh Duong, after arriving in the United States with her family, eventually attended high school in Maryland, graduating with honors. She studied engineering at the University of Maryland, graduating with a BS in both chemical engineering and computer science. Following graduation Anh worked as a chemical engineer at the Naval Surface Warfare Center–Indian Head Division (NSWC-IHD). Her specialty was explosives development. Following the 9/11 attacks, Anh headed a team that developed a thermobaric bomb capable of penetrating deep caves. The highly effective weapon was delivered in sixty-seven days, earning Anh the nickname "Bomb Lady." She has since served as the NSWC-IHD's director of science and technology. Anh is currently director for the Borders and Maritime Security Division in the Department of Homeland Security Science and Technology Directorate. She lives in Laurel, Maryland.

Robert Heym, following his naval service, attended Louisiana State University, graduating summa cum laude as a mechanical engineer. Heym had a long career in the aerospace industry. Although retired from the Boeing Corporation, he still works for that firm as a contract engineer and lives in Hartselle, Alabama.

Dam Thuy Nguyen Hugo, after leaving the Fort Indiantown Gap refugee camp, taught in Texas and Michigan before teaching at an adult education center in Arlington, Virginia. She then became the YMCA's director of community services for metropolitan Washington, D.C., working with refugees. She was selected in 1985 to attend the World Conference on Women held in Nairobi, Kenya. *Washingtonian* magazine recognized her in 1989 as one of the "Washingtonians of the Year." She retired from the YMCA after twenty-six years there and resides in McLean, Virginia.

Paul Jacobs retired from the Navy in 1984 as a captain after commanding three ships and serving as the U.S. Navy's director of undersea surveillance. He is now the president/CEO of Veteran Resources Corporation in Fairfax, Virginia.

Robert Lemke retired from the Navy after twenty-two years of service. He then worked in ship repair and shipbuilding. In his retirement he works as a volunteer aiding children in Baja California, Mexico. He has his home near San Diego, California.

Gerald McClellan left the Navy in late 1975 and worked for the Chevron Corporation for thirty years. He retired in 2007 and lives in Riverside, California.

Richard McKenna served twenty-eight years in the Navy during which time he was XO of the battleship USS *New Jersey* and had three afloat commands. He is currently executive director of the Marine Exchange of Southern California, the de facto operations center for both the Port of Los Angeles and the Port of Long Beach.

Ba Van Nguyen, upon retirement from the Boeing Aircraft Company, decided to go back to Vietnam. He eventually returned to the United States and died in June 2013.

Miki Nguyen resides in Woodinville, Washington, with his wife and three children. He works for AT&T Wireless.

Nho Nguyen retired from Boeing after nearly twenty-five years. She went back to Vietnam with her husband, Ba, but then returned with him to the United States. She currently resides in Redmond, Washington.

Joseph Pham, also known as Pham Xuan Vinh, worked as an ESL (English as a Second Language) instructor, a bilingual columnist, a court interpreter and translator, and an author. He is now retired and makes his home in Seattle, Washington.

Thanh Pham, after leaving the Fort Indiantown Gap refugee center, worked as a cabinetmaker before attending Wilkes College in Wilkes-Barre, Pennsylvania. Upon graduation he took a job as an electrical field engineer for the Harris Corporation in Syosset, New York, a company specializing in navigational systems. Pham then was employed as an electrical engineer and software designer for Aeronautical Radio, Incorporated (ARINC) in Annapolis, Maryland. He retired in 2006 before resuming work as a software developer for MedAssurant, a health-care data management firm. He resides in Annapolis, Maryland.

Frederick "Rick" Sautter retired after serving twenty-four years in the Navy. He was then director of a two-hundred-bed inpatient treatment facility for alcoholism and drug abuse. He is currently the president/CEO of Clarity Enterprises, Inc., in Westlake Village, California.

Donald Swain, after his service on board *Kirk*, conducted high-altitude mountain combat search-and-rescue missions, many of which took place in Yosemite National Park. His Navy career then took him to the South Pole, where he worked with the National Science Foundation. Swain also flew with the Royal New Zealand Air Force. After a last command with the Naval Reserve Center in Huntsville, Alabama, he left the Navy for a year, returned as a TAR (Training and Administration of Reserves), and retired from the Navy with nearly twenty-five years of service. He is currently a police officer in Scottsdale, Arizona.

Lan Tran resides in Long Beach, California, and has been working for the Social Security Administration for more than twenty years. After leaving the Philippines she was transported to Guam where she gave birth to a girl, Tien. In keeping with Captain Jacobs' request, Lan named her new daughter Tran Nguyen Kirk Giang Tien. Her daughter's first name, Giang Tien, means "angel from the sky."

Tien Tran, daughter of Lan Tran, is the owner of Transit Events & Good Taste Catering, based in Los Angeles. The event production and special events catering company accommodates corporate clients in the lifestyle marketing industry.

Erich von Marbod, immediately after the war, returned to Washington, where he took charge of all Department of Defense support for the resettlement of Indochina refugees and served on the Presidential Task Force headed by Julia Taft, director of the Interagency Task Force on Indochina Refugees. He continued service as principal deputy assistant secretary of defense and then became director of the Defense Security Assistance Agency. Von Marbod saw service in Iran, becoming the senior representative of the U.S. Defense Department in that country before the Iranian revolution in 1979. He currently lives in Gainesville, Virginia.

USS *Kirk* (DE/FF-1087) served the U.S. Navy until her decommissioning in 1993. The former destroyer escort/frigate operates today in the Republic of China Navy [Taiwan] under the name *Fen Yang* (934). She is homeported in Keelung, Taiwan. Close examination of the warship's transom still reveals the raised weld outlining her original name.

Men of USS *Kirk* (DE-1087)

OFFICERS

Cdr. Paul Jacobs	Lt. (jg) Scott Olin
Lt. Cdr. Richard McKenna	Lt. (jg) Scott Steele
Lt. Jerry Kolman	Lt. (jg) Donald Swain
Lt. (jg) Edward Daugherty	Ens. Bruce Davidson
Lt. (jg) Hugh Grant	Ens. Robert Pennell
Lt. (jg) Michael Craig	Lt. Garry Cassat
Lt. (jg) Ellsworth Humes	Lt. (jg) Nathaniel Grissom
Lt. Frederick Sautter Jr.	Lt. (jg) John McAllister

Ens. Lance Mynderse
Lt. (jg) Allan Porter
Lt. Louis Arcuri
Ens. Craig Compiano

Lt. Hugh Doyle
Ens. Steven Wesco
Lt. (jg) John Pine

ENLISTED PERSONNEL

OSC David Burlison
EWC John Willoughby
OS1 Terrence Schultz
OS2 Mark Bertrand
OS2 James Bongaard
EW3 Paul Lawless II
OS3 Peter Burinskas
EW3 George Kiddie
OS3 William Norman
OS3 Thomas Oeding
EW3 Jay Tuttle
OS3 Eugene Varvi
OSSN Daniel Jackson
OSSN Peter Schermerhorn
OSSN Daniel Scott
OSSN John Shuman
OSSN John Sullivan
OSSN Todd Thedell
OS1 George Adkins
OS1 Jerome Biever
ETC Donald Legrand
ETR Alexander Gozdan
ETR2 Michael Manthe
ETR2 Glen Tahbonemah
ET3 Jack Cabana
ET3 Luther McCaig
ETRSA Joseph Malone
ETRSN Kenneth Albert
RMC Lorenzo Gassaway
SM1 Herbert Kenway
SM1 James Sackett
RM2 Charles Fowler II

RM2 Charlie Ingram
RM3 Thomas Condelles
RM3 Frank Towns
SMSN Curtis Hackney
RMSN Carl Henry
SMSN John Janecka
RMSN Robert Midkiff
SN Clarence Neal Jr.
SMSA John Yzaguirre
RM2 Gregory Harkins
RM2 Thomas Weippert
ADJ2 Richard Fisher
ADJ2 Juan Pavo
AX2 Steven See
AE3 Patrick Christian
AW3 Donald Cox
AX3 Kenneth Ferrell
AE3 Danny McClure
AW3 Michael Washington
AN George Geiger III
AN David Hyson
AN Gerald McClellan
AN Robert Willingham
ADJC Glen Bingham
AMH1 Douglas Ainsworth
AT1 Robert Byrnes
YNC William Behres
HMC Stephen Burwinkel
PN1 Thomas Ronan
QM2 John Carter
QM2 James Schwan
QM3 Mark Armstrong

HM3 Mark Falkenberg
PC3 Charles Kalb
YN3 Frank Soderborg
QMSN William Arenz
SN Larry Gonzales
PNSN Mark Thomas
QMSA Steven Tissot
BMC Andrew Smith
BM1 Henry Troy
BM2 Paul Dufrene
SN David Mikesell
SN Kenneth Prescott
SN Mathew Workman
SA Tyrone Bruner
SA Mark Bymaster
SA Dennis Carney
SA Joseph Chavez
SA Clarence Cunningham Jr.
SA Ricardo Dinoso
SA Albery Efferson
SA Zane Fleck
SA Santos Gomez
SA Dennis Hudson
SA Charles Justus
SA Larry Lashley
SA Eddie Lopez
SA Edilberto Peralta Jr.
SA Carl Richardson
SA Gerald Savannah
FA Langston Smith
SA Curtis Tatum
SA Raymond Wilburn
SN William Daniels
SR Stephen Kling
SR Billy Skaggs
GMGCS Harvey Dilulo
FTGCS David Johnson
FTGC Lyle Baker
FTG2 John Wahlman Jr.

GMG3 Timothy Clancy
FTG3 Walter Johnson
GMG3 Carl Morgan
GMG3 Jack Sanders
GMG3 Gary Sanvig
FTGSN Frederick Roberts
GMGSN Mitchell Rogers
FTG1 Norman Moore
GMG3 Russell Benison
STGCS Joseph Benenati
GMT1 Thomas Dixon
STG1 Richard Lee
STG1 Coy Meadows
STG1 Theodore Sievert III
STG2 Mark Dallner
TM2 Larry McDaniels
STG2 William Mundy
STG2 Michael Riche
STG2 Jeffrey Rohrbaugh
STG2 Daniel Weller
STG2 James Wimbrow
STG3 Michael Closs
GMT3 Bertram Denton
STG3 Emery Kirk
SN William Cutler Jr.
SN William Hancock Jr.
GMTSA Richard Bankston
STGSA Danny Pallas
STGSA Dennis Troxell
STG1 Daniel Lucero
STG2 Wayne Brakensiek
STG3 Raymond Paul
STGSA James Knox
SKCS Robert Lewis Jr.
MS1 Merino Buenaflor
SH1 Nicholas Colaneri
DK1 Michael Edwards
DK1 Victoriano Gonzales
MS1 Cesar Olaes

MS1 Serafin Sobocor
SK1 Jeffrey Swan
MS2 Al Alinsunurin
MS2 Fely Eugenio
MS2 Leonardo Garde
SK2 Robert Hills
MS2 Alfonso Lumaban
SK2 Charles Riggs
MS3 William Burgwald
SH3 Robert Chamberlain
MS3 Manuel Elefane
SH3 Nicanor Estandarte
SH3 Gerald Harrison
MS3 Mark Langel
SH3 Terrance O'Neill
SH3 Ronnie Patrick
MS3 Romeo Poblete
MS3 Loras Reiter
SN Ricardo Flores Jr.
SHSN David Manselle
MSSN Gregory Morse
SKSA Bennie Logan
SKSA Randall Richardson
MMC Raul Renteria
EMC Winston Wells
MR1 Pascual Deomampo
HT1 Eugene Hassell
EM1 Quitin Mabanta
IC1 Thomas Powell
EN1 Dennis Weston
EM2 Patrick Bell
EN2 Jon Johnson
EM2 Dawilo Jose
HT2 Gregory Markert
EN2 Larry Mynatt
IC2 Terry Sitler
MM2 James Stombaugh
MM3 Paul Bare
EM3 Jacob Borillo

EM3 Joe Boyd
EM3 Jose Caldron
HT3 Millard Eldred
MM3 Ferdinand Flores
HT3 Steven Hauencraft
EM3 David Martinez
HT3 Roy Reger
EM3 Darrel Risinger
EM3 John Torres
HT3 Donald Weese
MMFN Howard "Kent" Chipman
FN Michael Abbot
FN Frederick Butler
ICFN Edward Cowart
FN Reginald Harrison
FN Joseph Hickey
FN Pedro Rocha
HTFA Russel Banna
HTFA John Licare
FA Tony Ong
ICFA Glen VanLeeuwen
HTTA Jeffrey Winter
MMC William Lemmon
MMC Larry Loughridge
MM2 William Boyles
MM2 Kim Eddy
MM2 Lonnie Glick
MM2 Stephen Iannazzo
MM2 Tony Pearce
MM2 Pedro Delmundo
MM3 James Berry
MM3 Kerry Boehle
MM3 Robert Heym
MM3 George Mendoza
MM3 Michael Puno
MM3 Marc Reichert
MM3 Kenneth Richardson
MMFN Jeffery Harris
MMFN Stephen Icenhower

MMFN Brad Nelson
MMFN Thomas Walton
MMFA Michael Gravitt
MMFA Douglas Miller
MMFA Larry Miller
MMFA William Miller
MMFA Thomas Swenson
MM2 Danny Needham
MM3 Charles Lavanaway
BTC John Gornto
BTC Wallace Michaelson
BT1 Carey Avery
BT1 Leon Franklin
BT2 James Batts
BT2 Allen Langteau
BT2 John Poole
BT3 Richard Lalonde
BT3 Robert Laser

BT3 Kevin Ryan
BT3 Jay Scarrow
BT3 Alan White
BT3 Curtis Williams
BT3 David Winkleblack
FN David Campbell
BTFN Jack Creutzberg
BTFN Bernard Hopkins
FN Eric Johnson
BTFN Gaylord Malone
BTFA Geroni Baniqued
BTFA John Barney
BTFA William Burbridge
BTFA James Didway
BTFA Gregory McCarty
FA Kevin Roach
BTFA Ramon Zamarripa
FA Victor Kovatch

DESTROYER SQUADRON (DESRON) 23 STAFF EMBARKED ON BOARD USS *KIRK*

Capt. Donald P. Roane
Lt. Cdr. John Loftus Jr.
Lt. Cdr. R. H. Fitzgerald
Lt. Lee Clark
Lt. Robert Moore
Lt. Robert Lemke

Lt. Charles Banellis
NCC Steven Schaffner
YN2 Clifton Carmody
YN1 Charles Montgomery
RMCS James Taylor

APPENDIX: RANKS AND RATES

Ranks

Adm.	Admiral
Capt.	Captain
Cdr.	Commander
CO	Commanding Officer
Commo.	Commodore
Ens.	Ensign
Lt. Cdr.	Lieutenant Commander
Lt. (jg)	Lieutenant (junior grade)
OOD	Officer of the Deck
XO	Executive Officer

Rates

ADJ2	Aviation Machinist's Mate Jet Engine Mechanic 2nd Class
ADJC	Chief Aviation Machinist's Mate Jet Engine Mechanic
AE3	Aviation Electrician's Mate 3rd Class
AMH1	Aviation Structural Mechanic (Hydraulics) 1st Class
AN	Airman
AT1	Aviation Electronics Technician 1st Class
AW3	Aviation Antisubmarine Warfare Operator 3rd Class
AX2	Aviation Antisubmarine Warfare Technician 2nd Class
AX3	Aviation Antisubmarine Warfare Technician 3rd Class
BM1	Boatswain's Mate 1st Class
BM2	Boatswain's Mate 2nd Class
BMC	Chief Boatswain's Mate
BT1	Boiler Technician 1st Class

BT2	Boiler Technician 2nd Class
BT3	Boiler Technician 3rd Class
BTC	Chief Boiler Technician
BTFA	Boiler Technician Fireman Apprentice
BTFN	Boiler Technician Fireman
DK1	Disbursing Clerk 1st Class
EM1	Electrician's Mate 1st Class
EM2	Electrician's Mate 2nd Class
EM3	Electrician's Mate 3rd Class
EMC	Chief Electrician's Mate
EN1	Engineman 1st Class
EN2	Engineman 2nd Class
ET3	Electronics Technician 3rd Class
ETC	Chief Electronics Technician
ETR	Electronics Technician (Radar)
ETR2	Electronics Technician (Radar) 2nd Class
ETRSA	Electronics Technician (Radar) Seaman Apprentice
ETRSN	Electronics Technician (Radar) Seaman
EW3	Electronic Warfare Technician 3rd Class
EWC	Chief Electronic Warfare Technician
FA	Fireman Apprentice
FN	Fireman
FTG	Fire Control Technician (Gun Fire Control)
FTGC	Chief Fire Control Technician (Gun Fire Control)
FTGCS	Senior Chief Fire Control Technician (Gun Fire Control)
FTGSN	Fire Control Technician (Gun Fire Control) Seaman
GMG3	Gunner's Mate (Guns) 3rd Class
GMGCS	Senior Chief Gunner's Mate (Guns)
GMGSN	Gunner's Mate (Guns) Seaman
GMT1	Gunner's Mate (Technician) 1st Class
GMT3	Gunner's Mate (Technician) 3rd Class
GMTSA	Gunner's Mate (Technician) Seaman Apprentice
HM3	Hospital Corpsman 3rd Class
HMC	Chief Hospital Corpsman
HT1	Hull Maintenance Technician 1st Class
HT2	Hull Maintenance Technician 2nd Class
HT3	Hull Maintenance Technician 3rd Class
HTFA	Hull Maintenance Technician Fireman Apprentice
IC1	Interior Communications Electrician 1st Class

IC2	Interior Communications Electrician 2nd Class
ICFA	Interior Communications Electrician Fireman Apprentice
ICFN	Interior Communications Electrician Fireman
MM2	Machinist's Mate 2nd Class
MM3	Machinist's Mate 3rd Class
MMC	Chief Machinist's Mate
MMFA	Machinist's Mate Fireman Apprentice
MMFN	Machinist's Mate Fireman
MR1	Machinery Repairman 1st Class
MS1	Mess Management Specialist 1st Class
MS2	Mess Management Specialist 2nd Class
MS3	Mess Management Specialist 3rd Class
MSSN	Mess Management Specialist Seaman
NCC	Chief Navy Counselor
OS1	Operations Specialist 1st Class
OS2	Operations Specialist 2nd Class
OS3	Operations Specialist 3rd Class
OSC	Chief Operations Specialist
OSSN	Operations Specialist Seaman
PC3	Postal Clerk 3rd Class
PN1	Personnelman 1st Class
PNSN	Personnelman Seaman
QM2	Quartermaster 2nd Class
QM3	Quartermaster 3rd Class
QMSA	Quartermaster Seaman Apprentice
QMSN	Quartermaster Seaman
RM2	Radioman 2nd Class
RM3	Radioman 3rd Class
RMC	Chief Radioman
RMCS	Senior Chief Radioman
RMSN	Radioman Seaman
SA	Seaman Apprentice
SH1	Ship's Serviceman 1st Class
SH3	Ship's Serviceman 3rd Class
SHSN	Ship's Serviceman Seaman
SK1	Storekeeper 1st Class
SK2	Storekeeper 2nd Class
SKCS	Senior Chief Storekeeper
SKSA	Storekeeper Seaman Apprentice

SM1	Signalman 1st Class
SMSA	Signalman Seaman Apprentice
SMSN	Signalman Seaman
SN	Seaman
SR	Seaman Recruit
STG1	Sonar Technician (Surface) 1st Class
STG2	Sonar Technician (Surface) 2nd Class
STG3	Sonar Technician (Surface) 3rd Class
STGCS	Senior Chief Sonar Technician (Surface)
STGSA	Sonar Technician (Surface) Seaman Apprentice
TM2	Torpedoman's Mate 2nd Class
YN1	Yeoman 1st Class
YN2	Yeoman 2nd Class
YN3	Yeoman 3rd Class
YNC	Chief Yeoman

NOTES

Preface

1. Jan K. Herman, *Navy Medicine in Vietnam: Oral Histories from Dien Bien Phu to the Fall of Saigon* (Jefferson, NC: McFarland, 2009).

Introduction

1. Telephone interview with Robert Lemke, April 29, 2009.
2. Ibid,
3. Ibid.
4. Interview with Paul Jacobs, Fairfax, VA, December 29, 2006.

Chapter 1. Man-of-War

1. Alan G. Kirk had also been amphibious commander during the 1943 Sicily landings, and after World War II he served as ambassador to Belgium, the Soviet Union, and China.
2. Until the U.S. Navy accepted the ship, her operation and security were still the responsibility of the builder, Avondale Shipyard, which technically still owned the ship.
3. The *Knox* class had two distinct subclasses: the *Knox* subclass (from DE-1052 through DE-1077) and the *Hewes* subclass (from DE-1078 through DE-1097). *Kirk* was really a *Hewes*-class ship. The difference was mainly in the propulsion plant, not the weapons systems. In June 1975 all DEs in both subclasses were redesignated "frigates" (FF).
4. As with the other *Hewes*-subclass DEs, the stateroom on *Kirk*'s port side under the bridge on the 01-level was designated a "flag" stateroom. Staterooms for flag staff were also on the 01-level in what was called "Officers' Country" when the ship was serving as a flagship.

Chapter 2. The Old Man

1. Interview with Paul Jacobs, Fairfax, VA, December 29, 2006.
2. Ibid.
3. Ibid.
4. Ibid.
5. Ibid.
6. U.S. Navy Officer Fitness Report, April 1959.
7. Interview with Paul Jacobs, Fairfax, VA.
8. Minesweepers had wooden hulls with bronze and stainless (nonmagnetic) steel fittings to minimize their magnetic signature. They had mine-locating sonar, and they were equipped to sweep for moored, bottom contact, magnetic, and acoustic mines.
9. U.S. Navy Officer Fitness Report, May 1967.
10. Interview with Paul Jacobs, Washington, DC, October 12, 2011.
11. Ibid.
12. Telephone interview with Richard Dobre, October 28, 2011.
13. Telephone interview with James Donovan, October 31, 2011.
14. Ibid.
15. Ibid.
16. Telephone interview with James McCulloch, October 31, 2011.
17. Interview with Paul Jacobs, Washington, DC.
18. Ibid.
19. Ibid.
20. Ibid.
21. Ibid.
22. Ibid.
23. Telephone interview with Richard McKenna, December 13, 2011.
24. A disciplinary hearing in which a CO hears and disposes of cases involving those in his or her command. The hearing might result in nonjudicial punishment.
25. Ibid.
26. A "snipe" is an enlisted person within an engineering rating. Those crew members with that specific rating work below the waterline in engineering main propulsion spaces. They include machinist's mates, boiler technicians, and electrician's mates.
27. Telephone interview with Robert Heym, November 29, 2011.
28. Ibid.
29. Ibid.
30. Interview with Paul Jacobs, Fairfax, VA.
31. Telephone interview with Robert Heym.
32. Ibid.
33. Ibid.

34. Telephone interview with Richard McKenna.
35. Interview with Paul Jacobs, Washington, DC.
36. Telephone interview with Robert Heym.
37. Ibid.
38. Interview with Paul Jacobs, Washington, DC.
39. Telephone interview with Hugh Doyle, January 29, 2007.

Chapter 3. Dunkirk in Reverse

1. Telephone interview with Hugh Doyle, January 29, 2007.
2. Ibid.
3. Interview with Paul Jacobs, Fairfax, VA, December 29, 2006.
4. Ibid.
5. Ibid.
6. Telephone interview with Bob Lemke, April 29, 2009.
7. Telephone interview with Hugh Doyle.
8. Daly later added that no intelligence had detected the movement of any North Vietnamese aircraft heading into South Vietnam. Furthermore, had the North Vietnamese attempted such a shift, it would have taken them several days to set up an infrastructure and necessary support organization that could have enabled aircraft to operate from Tan Son Nhut and Bien Hoa air bases. "From the 28th through the 30th, there simply was not enough time for them to get set up. It was no worry to me."
9. Telephone interview with Daniel Daly, August 10, 2011.
10. Telephone interview with Richard McKenna, December 13, 2011.
11. Telephone interview with Hugh Doyle.
12. Telephone interview with Ray Addicott, August 27, 2010.
13. The heroic evacuation of British, French, Polish, and Belgian troops from the beaches of Dunkirk, France, in May–June 1940: during the nine-day operation, an estimated 338,000 Allied soldiers were rescued by ships and hundreds of small boats that had crossed the North Sea from southeastern England.
14. Telephone interview with Kent Chipman, March 3, 2009.
15. *The Lucky Few: The Story of USS* Kirk (documentary), Navy Medicine Support Command, Visual Information Directorate, U.S. Navy, 2010.
16. Telephone interview with Ray Addicott.
17. Telephone interview with Hugh Doyle.
18. *The Lucky Few: The Story of USS* Kirk.
19. Telephone interview with Daniel Daly.
20. Telephone interview with Hugh Doyle.
21. *Kirk*'s LAMPS (Light Airborne Multi-Purpose System) helicopter was down with a faulty speed-decreaser gearbox on one of its engines and was in the hangar

at the forward end of the ship's relatively small flight deck. With the telescoping hangar extended, useable deck space for landing had been reduced to 50 by 38 feet.

22. *The Lucky Few: The Story of USS* Kirk.
23. Ibid.
24. Telephone interview with Richard McKenna.
25. Telephone interview with Donald Cox, April 25, 2007.
26. Telephone interview with Gerald McClellan, November 24, 2010.
27. Ibid.
28. *The Lucky Few: The Story of USS* Kirk.
29. Ibid.
30. Ibid.
31. The crew of USS *Cook*, which was also receiving South Vietnamese Hueys, devised a solution to their nonskid deck problem. "The boatswain's mates had come up with a three-inch steel pipe," XO Ray Addicott stated, "and when a helo would land, we'd rock it up onto the steel pipe and roll it off the flight deck to clear the deck for the next one."
32. Telephone interview with Gerald McClellan.
33. Telephone interview with Kent Chipman, March 3, 2009.
34. Interview with Paul Jacobs, Washington, DC, October 12, 2011.
35. Telephone interview with Craig Compiano, January 23, 2009.
36. Telephone interview with Kent Chipman.
37. Ibid.
38. Telephone interview with Craig Compiano.
39. Telephone interview with Hugh Doyle.
40. Telephone interview with Craig Compiano.
41. *The Lucky Few: The Story of USS* Kirk.
42. Ibid.
43. Telephone interview with Hugh Doyle.

Chapter 4. A Ride out of the War

1. *The Lucky Few: The Story of USS* Kirk (documentary), Navy Medicine Support Command, Visual Information Directorate, U.S. Navy, 2010.
2. Ibid.
3. Ibid.
4. Ba Van Nguyen, undated and unpublished account of escape from Saigon.
5. Ibid.
6. *The Lucky Few: The Story of USS* Kirk.
7. Ba Van Nguyen.
8. *The Lucky Few: The Story of USS* Kirk.
9. Ba Van Nguyen.

10. Ibid.
11. Ibid.
12. Telephone interview with Kent Chipman, March 3, 2009.
13. Ibid.
14. Ibid.
15. Ibid.
16. *The Lucky Few: The Story of USS* Kirk.
17. Telephone interview with Hugh Doyle, January 29, 2007.
18. *The Lucky Few: The Story of USS* Kirk.
19. Telephone interview with Hugh Doyle.
20. Telephone interview with Donald Swain, July 30, 2009.
21. Telephone interview with Hugh Doyle.
22. *The Lucky Few: The Story of USS* Kirk.
23. Ibid.
24. Telephone interview with Richard McKenna, December 13, 2011.

Chapter 5. Last Gunship from Saigon

1. Telephone interview with John Bowman, September 10, 2010.
2. Ibid.
3. Ibid.
4. Ibid.
5. Ibid.
6. Ibid.
7. Ibid.
8. Ibid.
9. Ibid.
10. Telephone interview with Hugh Doyle, January 29, 2007.
11. Ibid.
12. Ibid.
13. Telephone interview with John Bowman.
14. Ibid.
15. Ibid.
16. Ibid.
17. Ibid.
18. Interview with Paul Jacobs, Fairfax, VA, December 29, 2006.
19. Telephone interview with John Bowman.

Chapter 6. Armitage

1. Telephone interview with Hugh Doyle, January 29, 2007.
2. Ibid.

3. Telephone interview with Richard McKenna, December 13, 2011.
4. Telephone interview with Hugh Doyle.
5. Hugh Doyle, *Edited Transcript of Lt. Hugh J. Doyle's Vietnam Evacuation Tapes, 2 May–6 May 1975.*
6. Telephone interview with Richard McKenna.
7. *The Lucky Few: The Story of USS* Kirk (documentary), Navy Medicine Support Command, Visual Information Directorate, U.S. Navy, 2010.
8. Telephone interview with Richard McKenna.
9. Interview with Richard Armitage, Arlington, VA, October 31, 2008.
10. Telephone interview with James Kelly, July 7, 2011.
11. Telephone interview with Lawrence Ropka, August 10, 2011.
12. Telephone interview with James Kelly.
13. Ibid.
14. Ibid.
15. Interview with Richard Armitage, Arlington, VA.
16. Telephone interview with James Kelly.
17. Telephone interview with Lawrence Ropka.
18. Interview with Erich von Marbod, Gainesville, VA.
19. Interview with Richard Armitage, Arlington, VA.
20. Telephone interview with James Kelly.
21. Interview with Richard Armitage, Arlington, VA.
22. Telephone interview with Kiem Do, January 6, 2008.
23. Interview with Erich von Marbod, Gainesville, VA, August 25, 2011.
24. Telephone interview with Richard Armitage, August 31, 2011.
25. Kiem Do and Julie Kane, *Counterpart: A South Vietnamese Naval Officer's War* (Annapolis, MD: Naval Institute Press, 1998), p. 201.
26. Interview with Erich von Marbod, Gainesville, VA.
27. Ibid.
28. Telephone interview with Richard Armitage.
29. Ibid.
30. Interview with Erich von Marbod, Gainesville, VA.
31. Interview with Richard Armitage, Arlington, VA.
32. Interview with Erich von Marbod, Gainesville, VA.
33. Interview with Richard Armitage, Arlington, VA.
34. Ibid.
35. Ibid.

Chapter 7. Vessels of Opportunity

1. Telephone interview with Joseph Pham, February 11, 2007.
2. Ibid.
3. Ibid.

4. Ibid.
5. Ibid.
6. Interview with Dam Thuy Nguyen Hugo, McLean, VA, October 27, 2009.
7. Hugh Doyle, *Edited Transcript of Lt. Hugh J. Doyle's Vietnam Evacuation Tapes, 2 May–6 May 1975.*
8. Ibid.
9. Interview with Dam Thuy Nguyen Hugo, McLean, VA.
10. Ibid.
11. Ibid.
12. Ibid.
13. Ibid.
14. Ibid.
15. Ibid.
16. Ibid.
17. Ibid.
18. Ibid.
19. Ibid.
20. Ibid.
21. Interview with Stephen Burwinkel, Pensacola, FL, December 16, 2008.
22. Ibid.
23. Interview with Dam Thuy Nguyen Hugo, McLean, VA.
24. Ibid.
25. Ibid.
26. Telephone interview with Lan Nguyen Tran, April 12, 2007.
27. Ibid.
28. Ibid.
29. Ibid.
30. Ibid.
31. Ibid.
32. Ibid.
33. Ibid.
34. *The Lucky Few: The Story of USS* Kirk (documentary), Navy Medicine Support Command, Visual Information Directorate, U.S. Navy, 2010.

Chapter 8. Con Son Rendezvous

1. *The Lucky Few: The Story of USS* Kirk (documentary), Navy Medicine Support Command, Visual Information Directorate, U.S. Navy, 2010.
2. Interview with Richard Armitage, Arlington, VA, October 31, 2008.
3. *The Lucky Few: The Story of USS* Kirk.
4. Ibid.
5. Ibid.

6. Ibid.
7. Hugh Doyle, *Edited Transcript of Lt. Hugh J. Doyle's Vietnam Evacuation Tapes, 2 May–6 May 1975.*
8. Telephone interview with Daniel Daly, August 10, 2011.
9. Ibid.
10. *The Lucky Few: The Story of USS* Kirk.
11. Interview with Paul Jacobs, Fairfax, VA, December 29, 2006.
12. Deck Log of USS *Kirk* (DE-1087), May 2, 1975 (College Park, MD: National Archives and Records Administration).
13. By this time, USS *Cook*, USS *Tuscaloosa*, USS *Abnaki*, USS *Deliver*, and USS *Lipan* had joined the formation, now consisting of thirty-eight U.S. and South Vietnamese ships.
14. Doyle, *Vietnam Evacuation Tapes, 2 May–6 May 1975.*
15. Ibid.
16. Ibid.
17. Ibid.
18. The Vietnamese navy patterned its special operations force after the U.S. Navy SEALs (Sea, Air, and Land teams).
19. Telephone interview with Frederick Sautter, March 2, 2009.
20. Ibid.
21. Doyle, *Vietnam Evacuation Tapes, 2 May–6 May 1975.*

Chapter 9. House Calls

1. *The Lucky Few: The Story of USS* Kirk (documentary), Navy Medicine Support Command, Visual Information Directorate, U.S. Navy, 2010.
2. Hugh Doyle, *Edited Transcript of Lt. Hugh J. Doyle's Vietnam Evacuation Tapes, 2 May–6 May 1975.*
3. Ibid.
4. Ibid.
5. Ibid.
6. Ibid.
7. *The Lucky Few: The Story of USS* Kirk.
8. Interview with Stephen Burwinkel, Pensacola, FL, December 16, 2008.
9. *The Lucky Few: The Story of USS* Kirk.
10. Interview with Stephen Burwinkel, December 16, 2008.
11. Ibid.
12. Ibid.
13. Ibid.
14. Ibid.
15. Ibid.
16. Ibid.
17. Ibid.

18. Burwinkel recalled the two seasoned helicopter pilots trying to ease the tension by having some amusement at his expense. Through his active headset, he heard the two pilots bantering in the cockpit.

"Gee, I wonder what this button does?"

"I have no idea. Let's push it and see what happens!"

One pilot then said, "Hey Doc, if something happens and we go in the water, you need to push yourself out the door, pull those cords on your Mae West, and you'll pop to the surface."

Taking them seriously, Burwinkel wondered what would become of his patient if they had to ditch.

19. Interview with Stephen Burwinkel, Pensacola, FL, January 23, 2007.
20. *The Lucky Few: The Story of USS* Kirk.
21. Telephone interview with Joseph Pham, February 11, 2007.
22. Telephone interview with Lan Nguyen Tran, April 12, 2007.
23. Ibid.
24. *The Lucky Few: The Story of USS* Kirk.
25. Ibid.
26. USS *Cook* also took on board several pregnant women, but "no babies were born on board—we had great hopes," recounted the ship's CO, Cdr. Jerry McMurry.
27. Interview with Stephen Burwinkel, December 16, 2008.
28. *The Lucky Few: The Story of USS* Kirk.
29. Ibid.
30. Telephone interview with Ray Addicott, August 27, 2010.
31. Telephone interview with Jerry McMurry, September 7, 2010.
32. Interview with Stephen Burwinkel, December 16, 2008.
33. Ibid.
34. *The Lucky Few: The Story of USS* Kirk.
35. Interview with Paul Jacobs, Fairfax, VA, December 29, 2006.
36. Interview with Erich von Marbod, Gainesville, VA, August 25, 2011.

Chapter 10. Destination Subic Bay

1. Hugh Doyle, *Edited Transcript of Lt. Hugh J. Doyle's Vietnam Evacuation Tapes, 2 May–6 May 1975.*
2. Ibid.
3. Ibid.
4. *The Lucky Few: The Story of USS* Kirk (documentary), Navy Medicine Support Command, Visual Information Directorate, U.S. Navy, 2010.
5. Ibid.
6. Ibid.
7. Ibid.
8. HQ-3 actually had ample freshwater but, as Doyle remembered, "They just couldn't figure out how to pump it. They got a crash course from my engineers

on how to line up a freshwater system, plus they got nearly all of *Kirk*'s potable water to boot."

9. *The Lucky Few: The Story of USS* Kirk.
10. Doyle, *Vietnam Evacuation Tapes, 2 May–6 May 1975*.
11. Ibid.
12. Ibid.
13. Telephone interview with Hugh Doyle, January 29, 2007.
14. *The Lucky Few: The Story of USS* Kirk.
15. Interview with Kimmy, Kim, Kimsa, and Pierre Le, Pensacola, FL, October 20, 2010.
16. Ibid.
17. *The Lucky Few: The Story of USS* Kirk.
18. Ibid.
19. Doyle, *Vietnam Evacuation Tapes, 2 May-6 May 1975*.
20. *The Lucky Few: The Story of USS* Kirk.
21. Ibid.
22. Telephone interview with Anh Duong, September 18, 2009.
23. Ibid.
24. Ibid.
25. Ibid.

Chapter 11. Diplomatic Crisis

1. Deck Log of USS *Kirk* (DE-1087), May 5, 1975 (College Park, MD: National Archives and Records Administration).
2. Telephone interview with Donald Cox, April 25, 2007.
3. Ibid.
4. Ibid.
5. Ibid.
6. Telephone interview with Todd Thedell, November 24, 2011.
7. Telephone interview with Donald Swain, July 30, 2009.
8. Ibid.
9. Ibid.
10. Telephone interview with Frederick Sautter, March 2, 2009.
11. Hugh Doyle, *Edited Transcript of Lt. Hugh J. Doyle's Vietnam Evacuation Tapes, 2 May–6 May 1975*.
12. Ibid.
13. *The Lucky Few: The Story of USS* Kirk (documentary), Navy Medicine Support Command, Visual Information Directorate, U.S. Navy, 2010.
14. Doyle, *Vietnam Evacuation Tapes, 2 May–6 May 1975*.
15. Ibid.
16. Interview with Erich von Marbod, Gainesville, VA, August 25, 2011.

17. William H. Sullivan, *Obbligato: Notes on a Foreign Service Career* (New York: W. W. Norton, 1984), p. 253.
18. Ibid., p. 254.
19. Telephone interview with Robert Lemke, April 29, 2009.
20. Ibid.
21. *The Lucky Few: The Story of USS* Kirk.
22. Ibid.
23. Ibid.
24. Ibid.
25. Interview with Dam Thuy Nguyen Hugo, McLean, VA, October 27, 2009.
26. *The Lucky Few: The Story of USS* Kirk.
27. Telephone interview with Donald Swain.
28. Telephone interview with Liem Bui, July 8, 2009.
29. Telephone interview with Thanh Pham, June 30, 2009.
30. Telephone interview with Donald Swain.
31. *The Lucky Few: The Story of USS* Kirk.
32. Telephone interview with Donald Swain.

Epilogue

1. *The Lucky Few: The Story of USS* Kirk (documentary), Navy Medicine Support Command, Visual Information Directorate, U.S. Navy, 2010.
2. Telephone interview with Joseph Pham, February 11, 2007.
3. Ibid.
4. Ibid.
5. Ibid.
6. Ibid.
7. Interview with Dam Thuy Nguyen Hugo, McLean, VA, October 27, 2009.
8. Ibid.
9. Ibid.
10. Ibid.
11. Ibid.
12. Ibid.
13. Telephone interview with Lan Nguyen Tran, April 12, 2007.
14. Ibid.
15. Ibid.
16. *The Lucky Few: The Story of USS* Kirk.
17. An archipelago of more than 750 reefs, islands, atolls, cays, and islets in the South China Sea.
18. Telephone interview with Thanh Pham, June 30, 2009.
19. Ibid.
20. Ibid.

21. Ibid.
22. Ibid.
23. *The Lucky Few: The Story of USS* Kirk.
24. Telephone interview with Robert Lemke, April 29, 2009.
25. *The Lucky Few: The Story of USS* Kirk.
26. Telephone interview with Todd Thedell, November 24, 2011.
27. Telephone interview with Robert Heym, November 29, 2011.
28. *The Lucky Few: The Story of USS* Kirk.
29. Ibid.
30. Telephone interview with Donald Cox, April 25, 2007.
31. Ibid.

Postscript

1. http://www.npr.org/series/129580052/the-uss-kirk-valor-at-the-vietnam-wars-end.

BIBLIOGRAPHY

Published Sources

Butler, David. *The Fall of Saigon*. New York: Simon and Schuster, 1985.

Daly, Daniel. "The Last Shot." *Mensa Bulletin*. Issue 536, July 2010.

Do, Kiem, and Julie Kane. *Counterpart: A South Vietnamese Naval Officer's War*. Annapolis, MD: Naval Institute Press, 1998.

Dunham, George R. *U.S. Marines in Vietnam: The Bitter End, 1973–1975*. Marine Corps Vietnam Operational Historical Series. Quantico, VA: Marine Corps Association, 1990.

Duong, Van Nguyen. *Tragedy of the Vietnam War: A South Vietnamese Officer's Analysis*. Jefferson, NC: McFarland, 2008.

Henderson, Charles. *Good Night Saigon*. New York: Berkley Publishing Group, 2005.

Herman, Jan K. *Navy Medicine in Vietnam: Oral Histories from Dien Bien Phu to the Fall of Saigon*. Jefferson, NC: McFarland, 2009.

Lim, Benito, and Maria Teresa Melgar, eds. *Asian Studies*. Quezon City: Asian Center, University of the Philippines, 1997.

Mann, James. *Rise of the Vulcans: The History of Bush's War Cabinet*. New York: Viking, 2004.

Marolda, Edward J. *By Sea, Air, and Land: An Illustrated History of the U.S. Navy and the War in Southeast Asia*. Washington, DC: Naval Historical Center, 1992.

Snepp, Frank. *Decent Interval*. New York: Vintage Books, 1977.

Sullivan, William H. *Obbligato: Notes on a Foreign Service Career*. New York: W.W. Norton, 1984.

Todd, Olivier. *Cruel April: The Fall of Saigon*. New York: W.W. Norton, 1990.

Unpublished Sources

Accident report relating to the loss of AH-1J Cobra, May 1975. Courtesy of John Bowman.

Cassat, Garry (USS *Kirk* Weapons Officer). Undated after action report.

A Closing History of the Thirty-First Aerospace Rescue and Recovery Squadron, 1 January 1975–30 June 1975. Prepared by 1st Lt. Joseph E. Kane, Squadron Historian.

Washington, DC: Air Force Historical Studies Office, Research and Analysis Division, Bolling AFB.

Deck Log of USS *Badger* (DE-1071), 1 May–4 May 1975. College Park, MD: National Archives and Records Administration.

Deck Log of USS *Blue Ridge* (LCC-19), 29 April–4 May 1975. College Park, MD: National Archives and Records Administration.

Deck Log of USS *Cook* (DE-1083), 28 April–7 May 1975. College Park, MD: National Archives and Records Administration.

Deck Log of USS *Deliver* (ARS-23), 4 May–7 May 1975. College Park, MD: National Archives and Records Administration.

Deck Log of USS *Flint* (AE-32), 29 April–4 May 1975. College Park, MD: National Archives and Records Administration.

Deck Log of USS *Kirk* (DE-1087), 22 April–10 May 1975. College Park, MD: National Archives and Records Administration.

Deck Log of USS *Mobile* (LKA-115), 28 April–7 May 1975. College Park, MD: National Archives and Records Administration.

Deck Log of USS *Vega* (AF-59), 28 April–7 May 1975. College Park, MD: National Archives and Records Administration.

Doyle, Hugh. *Edited Transcript of Lt. Hugh J. Doyle's Vietnam Evacuation Tapes*, 2 May–6 May 1975.

Heym, Robert. "My Personal Growth Agreement Conference Story," September 27, 2004.

http://www.npr.org/series/129580052/the-uss-kirk-valor-at-the-vietnam-war-5-end

McMurry, Jerry. Notes, 17 April–7 May 1975.

Mission Report of the Thirty-First Aerospace Rescue and Recovery Squadron, 5 May 1975. Washington, DC: Air Force Historical Studies Office, Research and Analysis Division, Bolling AFB.

Nguyen, Ba Van. Account of escape from Saigon. (n.d.) Courtesy of Miki Nguyen.

U.S. Navy Officer Fitness Report. (Paul Jacobs) April 1959.

U.S. Navy Officer Fitness Report. (Paul Jacobs) May 1967.

USS *Kirk* Cruise Book (WESTPAC 1975).

USS *Kirk* Familygram. April 1975.

INDEX

ABOUT THE AUTHOR

JAN K. HERMAN was chief historian of the Navy Medical Department from 1979 to 2012 and also curator of the Old Naval Observatory located in Washington, D.C.'s Foggy Bottom neighborhood. He was editor in chief of *Navy Medicine*, the journal of the Navy Medical Department, for thirty years. Since 2000 he has written and produced documentaries for the U.S. Navy highlighting its medical service during World War II, the Korean War, and the Vietnam War. *The Lucky Few*, a documentary about the closing days of the Vietnam War, provided the stimulus to create this companion book.

Herman has authored more than fifty articles and monographs plus five other books. As a lecturer he has spoken to many audiences across the United States, focusing on military medicine, nineteenth-century astronomy, and medical aspects of World War II in the Pacific.

In his retirement, he enjoys building ship models, collecting and shooting antique firearms, and walking and talking history.

The Naval Institute Press is the book-publishing arm of the U.S. Naval Institute, a private, nonprofit, membership society for sea service professionals and others who share an interest in naval and maritime affairs. Established in 1873 at the U.S. Naval Academy in Annapolis, Maryland, where its offices remain today, the Naval Institute has members worldwide.

Members of the Naval Institute support the education programs of the society and receive the influential monthly magazine *Proceedings* or the colorful bimonthly magazine *Naval History* and discounts on fine nautical prints and on ship and aircraft photos. They also have access to the transcripts of the Institute's Oral History Program and get discounted admission to any of the Institute-sponsored seminars offered around the country.

The Naval Institute's book-publishing program, begun in 1898 with basic guides to naval practices, has broadened its scope to include books of more general interest. Now the Naval Institute Press publishes about seventy titles each year, ranging from how-to books on boating and navigation to battle histories, biographies, ship and aircraft guides, and novels. Institute members receive significant discounts on the Press's more than eight hundred books in print.

Full-time students are eligible for special half-price membership rates. Life memberships are also available.

For a free catalog describing Naval Institute Press books currently available, and for further information about joining the U.S. Naval Institute, please write to:

Member Services
U.S. Naval Institute
291 Wood Road
Annapolis, MD 21402-5034
Telephone: (800) 233-8764
Fax: (410) 571-1703
Web address: www.usni.org